CHINA
AS A LEADER OF THE
WORLD ECONOMY

CHINA
AS A LEADER OF THE
WORLD ECONOMY

GREGORY C CHOW

Princeton University, USA

 World Scientific

NEW JERSEY · LONDON · SINGAPORE · BEIJING · SHANGHAI · HONG KONG · TAIPEI · CHENNAI

Published by

World Scientific Publishing Co. Pte. Ltd.

5 Toh Tuck Link, Singapore 596224

USA office: 27 Warren Street, Suite 401-402, Hackensack, NJ 07601

UK office: 57 Shelton Street, Covent Garden, London WC2H 9HE

Library of Congress Cataloging-in-Publication Data
Chow, Gregory C., 1929–
   China as a leader of the world economy / Gregory C. Chow.
   p. cm.
   ISBN 13-9789814368797 (hardcover)
   ISBN 10-9814368792 (hardcover)
   ISBN 13-9789814368803 (pbk.)
   ISBN 10-9814368806 (pbk.)
   1. International economic relations. 2. China--Economic conditions--2000–
3. China--Economic policy--2000–   4. China--Foreign economic relations.
   HC427.95 .C489 2011
   337.51

                        2011033280

British Library Cataloguing-in-Publication Data
A catalogue record for this book is available from the British Library.

Typeset by Stallion Press
Email: enquiries@stallionpress.com

Printed in Singapore by World Scientific Printers.

Preface

China as a leader of the world economy is perhaps one of the most important development of the 21st century. The main purpose of this book is to provide up-to-date analysis of the subject as contained in my recently published essays. Unlike chapters in a textbook, each chapter here is self-contained and some repetition of material is unavoidable. By reading these essays the reader will gain an understanding of the way that the Chinese economy functions.

There are four parts of this book dealing respectively with China's economic institutions, economic issues, economic policies and quantitative economic studies. The essays are not technical except for some in Part 4. Most have appeared in Chinese in my column in *China Business News*, a popular daily newspaper in China.

Chapter 1 is an introduction providing an overview of the Chinese economy. Chapter 2 explains the government, the entrepreneurs and the ordinary citizens and workers as three important players. The following chapters discuss the nature of Chinese capitalism, economic planning, the role of economists in economic development, topics parallel to those discussed in the well-known book *Free to Choose* by Milton and Rose Friedman, differences between the Chinese and American economies as reflecting their cultural differences, recent outflow of Chinese capital, the economic relation between Brazil and China, India's model of rapid economic development, Russia's economic growth and a comparison of economic developments of Taiwan and China.

Part 2 begins with a summary of problems facing the Chinese economy. Other issues include directions for economics education research, important lessons I have learned by studying the Chinese economy, some US economic problems by comparison, and whether the low rate of aggregate consumption will increase in the future.

Economic policies is an interesting subject. Part 3 covers policies for university education, for improving efficiency of state-owned enterprises, the open door policy, policy to stop inflation, China's aging population originated from the one-child policy and China's environmental policy. Part 4 provides several studies on the Chinese macro-economy and on the co-movement of prices of stocks traded in the Shanghai and New York Stock Exchanges.

I would like to acknowledge with thanks financial support from the Gregory C Chow Econometric Research Program of Princeton University for research on which some of the articles in this book is based. I would also like to acknowledge the excellent editorial work provided by Ms. Tang Yu of World Scientific that has improved this book substantially.

The Chinese economy is a fascinating subject to me. I am pleased to write down some of my thoughts about it with the hope that readers will provide me with critical comments.

Gregory C Chow
Princeton, New Jersey
June, 2011

Contents

PART 1

Economic Institutions

CHAPTER 1

Introduction: An Overview of China's Economy

After explaining why the Chinese economy has managed to grow so rapidly this introduction points out China's economic strength, compares its market institutions with the US institutions, discusses some of its short-term and long-term economic policies and finally reviews China's role as a leader in the world economy.

1.1. How did China Manage to Grow so Rapidly?

China's rapid economic growth since the government decided to introduce reform in the early 1980s to change from a planned economy to a market economy is not a miracle but follows a basic law in economics. As I have pointed out in previous writings, there are three fundamental factors contributing to rapid economic growth. These are having an abundance of high-quality human capital, having a set of functioning market institutions and being in an early stage of development that enables the economy to catch up rapidly. These factors also explain the rapid economic growth of Japan before and after World War II, and of Hong Kong, Singapore, Taiwan and South Korea, known as the four dragons in East Asia, during the 1960s to early 1980s. In recent years India provides another example if we explain its earlier failure to grow rapidly by its failure to practice a market economy with a system that did not allowed free entry to potentially able entrepreneurs. Developed economies do not grow

3

rapidly because they cannot frog leap by adopting new technologies from the economically most advanced economies.

These three factors are not only necessary but sufficient if we attribute any failure to grow rapidly to the lack of human capital. Some observers attribute China's rapid economic growth to the able leaders in the Chinese government or the policies of gradualism and experimentation but these can be subsumed under the factor of human capital. Political stability may be said to be another factor but it is subsumed under a "functioning" market institutions. Political instability can disrupt the functioning of market institutions.

For three decades economic reform was the main topic in discussions of the Chinese economy. Today an equally important or perhaps a more important topic is entrepreneurship that propels China's economic changes and innovations. This is so because China has already achieved sufficient success in economic reform and has been recognized as a leader of the world economy. The recognition is seen in the term G2 that refers to the United States and China in economic and political discourse. The topic of entrepreneurship is the subject of the leading chapter in Chow (2010).

If the three factors are sufficient for rapid growth, one can predict that China's rapid growth, say in the order of 8% in GDP per year, will continue for at least another decade because these three factors will remain in place. The third factor will disappear gradually. China is a large country. The coastal provinces have developed more rapidly than other provinces mainly because they have higher quality human capital. The less developed provinces in the interior still have much room to grow.

1.2. China's Economic Strength

China is a member of G2 for good reasons. First of all, its GDP as measured in purchasing power parity terms will exceed that of the US in this decade. To make such a projection I begin with the International Monetary Fund's estimate of the Chinese GDP of 10.1 trillion US dollars in terms of purchasing power parity in 2010 as compared with the US GDP of 14.6 trillion. This makes China's

GDP equal to 0.692 of the US GDP. The World Bank has provided a similar estimate. (See *New York Times*, Jan 15, 2011). To make a projection from 2010 forward, assuming that the US real GDP will grow as much as 3.5% per year and the Chinese real GDP will grow at only 8% per year and raising the ratio $(1.080/1.035) = 1.1178$ to the 9th power gives 1.4667. When 0.692 is multiplied by this number, the result is slightly larger than one. Hence, by 2019 China's GDP will just exceed the US GDP. Although in per capita terms China's GDP will be much smaller, total output is a more useful measure of the economic strength of a country. The amounts of exports and imports, of foreign investment and foreign economic assistance are measures of economic power that depend on total output.

By 2011, China's economy already has other signs of its economic dominance. In technology it has the fastest supercomputer. A *New York Times* article on January 2, 2011 (p. C3) reported that in 2011 China will file more patents than the US, and the Chinese government has issued a target of filing 2 million patents in 2015, increasing from only 600,000 in 2009. In terms of the production of alternative energy, it is the world's largest producer of wind energy, nuclear energy and solar panels. Consumer goods produced by China flood the world market. Chinese tourists are seen travelling all over the world and making expensive purchases. From mostly receiving investment from other countries China has increased its investment abroad rapidly, in a process to catch up with the former.

1.3. Comparing China's Market Institutions with the US

The housing bubble and the ensuing economic downturn beginning in 2008 have revealed the institutional weaknesses of the American economy. US financial institutions and consumers were allowed to take too much risk. In the trading of financial derivatives and the financing of the purchase of new homes American financial institutions took gamble without sufficient capital. Consumers used credit cards to make purchases excessively and were able to purchase houses without any down payment. Such practices led to an economic downturn and subsequent government legislation to regulate such risky practices. But the effectiveness of the new regulations is still uncertain.

China does not have the above institutional weaknesses because the government's reform of financial institutions has been gradual and cautious. Chinese financial institutions are not allowed to take such high risks as the US institutions. Chinese consumers cannot use credit cards without sufficient deposit, nor can they purchase houses without a down payment. In addition the Chinese consumers are by tradition more thrifty.

Differences in economic institutions between China and the US can be explained by cultural differences in the two countries. Americans believe in individualism. The Chinese believe in collectivism. Americans believe in the Jeffersonian doctrine that the government is the best that governs the least. They distrust the government. By tradition the Chinese respect the government and government officials. The Chinese also respect authority. Although Americans distrust the government, they respect the law and are more law abiding than the Chinese. Confucianism puts less emphasis on obeying the law than on being guided by one's own moral judgment which may result in an appeal to authority. In many respects America is ruled by law and China is ruled by people. Many Americans believe that the government is the problem. The Chinese believe that the government is the solution to many problems. In America, businessmen avoid government intervention while they take risks. In China, businessmen make profit by cooperating with the government and the government officials.

In the course of rapid economic development in recent decades, profit seeking by Chinese entrepreneurs has served as an engine for growth. Chinese bureaucracy is a part of China's market economy as it facilitates the work of the entrepreneurs. Profit seeking in China propels growth but it does not affect adversely the entire system by excessive risk taking. Chinese financial institutions are not allowed to be too big to fail while profit seeking in American financial institutions has created economic instability.

Illegal profit seeking in China can harm many individuals such as the selling of false medicine and food products, but it does not seriously disturb the functioning of the entire economy. Risk taking involving very large sums of money in American is legal but has disrupted the functioning of the entire market economy. If so, by introducing new legislation to restrict the behavior of businessmen, the US government may not have succeeded in preventing future financial problems because there are new ways to get around the new laws. After the current economic downturn US financial institutions have not changed their behavior and have remained on top. The cooperation of Chinese bureaucrats with Chinese entrepreneurs may have contributed to economic growth but it has also involved extensive corruption. Corruption can create serious social instability and the Chinese Communist Party and the Chinese government have tried very hard to stop it but only with a limited degree of success.

Insofar as different countries establish different market institutions based on their own cultural heritage, one may question the use of a "China model" for other developing countries to follow. Other developing countries have their own social and cultural characteristics that should determine their own effective market institutions for the promotion of economic development. Just as China need not follow the "Washington consensus" on economic development, other developing countries need not follow the "China model" for their own development. Of course there may be elements in the "China model" useful for the economic development of other countries.

The US is enjoying its democratic government that allows for much more freedom and rights for the citizens, while China is practicing a one-party rule with citizens enjoying less political freedom and human rights. However, the Chinese government is much more efficient in making decisions affecting the national economy. A decision to increase government expenditures during an economic slowdown can be made by top government officials in China, while it is subject to debate in the US Congress. Political interests on the part of the President and of members of Congress affect economic policies of the US as politicians are concerned about the next election.

Since 9/11, 2001 the US has waged its war against terrorism. It has been fighting two wars in Iraq and in Afghanistan and the end is not in sight. The war against terrorism has used up much economic resource, human and non-human, and increased the US government debt, both affecting the functioning of the US as a leader of the world economy while China is gaining ground as a leader.

Furthermore, Chinese government officials are cooperating with Chinese entrepreneurs in investing abroad and in spreading the country's economic influence world wide. The US government is often taking an opposite side to business interests. President Obama, being a Democrat, is not well trusted by some members of the US business community although he has made special attempts to be friendly to big business. The Chinese government has encouraged competition among Chinese enterprises not only in domestic economic development but also in investment abroad and acquiring foreign assets. Competition has made the processes of domestic economic development and the extension of China's economic power abroad more efficient.

1.4. China's Short-Term Economic Policies

China is having inflation today. Recently the State Council sent orders to provincial and city governments to control prices. Generally speaking, the use of price control is not an effective way to control inflation. One can recall that in 1961, during the period of central planning, China had price control but the retail price index went up by 16.2% according to *China Statistical Yearbook*. The main reason for inflation is the rapid increase in money supply relative to real GDP. In 1961, real GDP was reduced by 30% because of the economic failure of the Great Leap Forward Movement. To slow down inflation the basic solution is to reduce the rate of increase in money supply relative to the rate of growth of GDP.

In April 14, 2010 I published an article in *China Business News* entitled "Can inflation be avoided?" In that article I provided statistical evidence from 1952 to 2009 to support a theory that inflation in China is determined by three important variables. The variables are the change in the ratio of money supply M to real GDP Y, inflation of the last year and the deviation of the price level in the last year from its equilibrium relation to the ratio of money supply to real GDP. From an estimated equation based on this theory, I projected inflation in 2010 and concluded: "The current policy of the People's Bank to slow down the increase in money supply has been correct and the Bank needs to continue to restrict the increase in M/Y in order to maintain a stable price level."

As reported by Reuters from Beijing on September 11, 2010, the annual growth in China's broad M2 measure of money supply was 19.2% in August compared with 17.6% in July and was above the forecast of 17.5%. Money supply as measured by M2 had increased by 29.7%, 27.7% and 26.0% (as compared with a year ago) respectively in Nov 2009, Dec 2009 and Jan 2010. Realizing the inflationary pressure generated by such large increases in money supply the People's Bank began in April 2010 to increase the interest rates and raise the reserve requirement for commercial banks several times but failed to slow down the increase of M2 to a satisfactory level.

The main reason for the increase in money supply outside the control of the People's Bank is the inflow of foreign exchange which was converted to RMB. The inflow of foreign exchange was due to the foreign trade surplus generated by an undervaluation of the RMB. The basic solution to the inflation problem is therefore the revaluation of the RMB to a substantially higher level to eliminate the trade surplus. This may require an increase of some 20% or perhaps an even larger amount.

The Chinese government has not raised the exchange rate of RMB substantially mainly because of the possible disadvantages of doing so. The main disadvantage was the reduction of certain exports which helped generate output and employment in China. However such disadvantages are outweighed by many advantages. The major advantages are two. The first is to solve the inflation problem as pointed out above. The inflation problem may be more serious in the future if money supply is not controlled properly. The second is to allow China to import more at lower prices (since the Chinese currency will have a higher value as compared with foreign currencies). This will allow China to buy more for domestic consumption and for capital formation to speed up economic growth. Because of the undervaluation of the RMB China has had trade surplus for many years and has accumulated over 3 trillion US dollar worth of foreign exchange reserves. This amount of hard-earned money is not effectively utilized because much of it has remained idle and a substantial amount is invested in US Treasury bonds yielding a low rate of interest.

I have suggested that the Chinese government spend a substantial amount of its foreign reserves to make purchases in the US. This would increase the supply of US dollar in the market where Chinese and US currencies are traded and thus increase the value of the RMB relative to the US dollar. China's foreign reserves can be used for many important purposes. I suggested using it for the government's strategy of Western development. In the 12th Five-Year Plan beginning in 2011, there are many important projects that can be financed by using China's foreign reserves.

The spending of foreign reserves can also help solve the problem of recession in the United States. In the US there is a high rate of unemployment. The rate remained as high as 9.6% for many months before it was even increased further to 9.8% in late 2010. The Federal Reserve increased money supply in early November by 400 billion dollars with the purpose of stimulating economic activities but was criticized by some knowledgeable economists as this policy would increase the already large debt of the American government. Too much government debt will affect the credibility of the US government and make it difficult to borrow the future. Increasing money supply will also cause inflation in the US in the future.

If China uses its foreign reserves to purchase American goods, it will increase aggregate demand in the US and thus help the American economy to recover from its current recession. The US government and the American people have criticized China for taking away jobs from the US. They said that imports from China replaced American goods that were domestically produced and led to lower production and higher unemployment in the US. The policy of buying American goods as suggested will have the opposite effects. Buying American goods by using China's foreign reserves will also reduce the debt of the US government, because much of China's foreign reserves is held in the form of US Treasury Bonds.

Although China's policy on setting the exchange rate of the RMB is based on its domestic economic considerations, the American government and people have criticized the Chinese government for maintaining a low exchange rate of the RMB in order to create an export surplus and harm the US. Once China raises its exchange rate such a criticism will be less convincing. Raising the exchange rate of RMB and increasing purchases in the US should be beneficial to both countries.

1.5. China's Long-Term Economic Policies

As China's economic power increased, its economic influence in Asia, Europe, South America, Africa and even the US has increased. China has established its foreign political and economic relations with other countries on the principle of mutual interests. A main objective of the US foreign policy in recent years has been to fight the war on terrorism. The US has also been promoting its ideas of human rights and democracy in other countries. Such policies are often not welcome.

In the mean time China has increased its investment abroad. Investing abroad is advantageous for China as Chinese capital seeks a higher rate of return and China is able to secure control of basic mineral and energy resources abroad. It is also advantageous to the host countries as it promotes their economic development through the inflow of Chinese human, financial and physical capital, technology and development knowhow. The Chinese government has cooperated with Chinese entrepreneurs in investing abroad. It allows competition among Chinese investors, making the investment process more efficient. Many developing countries welcome China's investment more than US investment, partly because the Chinese have accumulated recent experience to promote rapid economic development that can be shared with them, while the US experience in economic development is much older and less relevant for rapid economic growth in the 21st century.

1.6. The Role of China as a Leader in the World Economy

Will a rising China be beneficial to the world? Since globalization in the form of flows of goods, capital, people and technology among nations is beneficial to the world, having China participate in globalization as an economic leader is beneficial to the world. However, there are recognizable disadvantages of globalization insofar as economic instability in one country can spread to other countries.

As China spreads its economic influence abroad, there have been signs recently of China's aggressions. Such aggressions have been criticized by China's neighbors. For example China's relation with Japan deteriorated in 2010 after it posed a strong stand against the Japanese government in the incident of a Chinese fishing boat colliding with a Japanese navy patrol boat in territorial water claimed by both countries. Even after the Japanese government released the captured Chinese fisherman, the Chinese government demanded an apology from the Japanese Premier. At about the same time, China was claiming territorial rights in South China sea against objections of Vietnam and some other neighbors. No matter which parties in such disputes had legitimate claims, one can observe the more aggressive stand in China's foreign policies which did not exist before.

As another sign of China's possible aggression, it is building up its military power. An article in the *New York Times* on January 6, 2011 reported China's military buildup, including jet fighters, aircraft carriers and anti-ship ballistic missile, called a "carrier-killer" for its potential to strike the big carriers. Such buildup will challenge the American military presence in the Western Pacific. As reported in the *New York Times* on January 9, 2011, US Defense Secretary Robert M. Gates said the Pentagon was investing in more weapons and technology in response to China's military presence.

Will China remain a peace loving nation as it spreads its economic power in the future? Before World War II most people considered the US a peace loving and not an expansionary country. After WWII as the US military and economic power increased American military forces are found stationed in all parts of the globe. The US has waged wars in Korea, Vietnam and in recent years in Iraq and Afghanistan. Would China engage in similar aggressive activities in the future once its power shall have increased greatly?

Both the United States and China are playing important roles as leaders of the world economy. Both have benefited other countries and have been criticized. At present, China does not have military forces stationed all over the world, although it has built up its military strength in jet fighters, aircraft carriers and ballistic missiles to counter the US military presence in Western Pacific. In the future, China's military posture is uncertain. Insofar as power can corrupt any government, we can only hope that the Chinese government will maintain a peaceful posture in accordance with its doctrine of peaceful rise.

References

Chow, Gregory C. (2007). *China's Economic Transformation*. Blackwell Publishers.

Chow, Gregory C. (2010). *Interpreting China's Economy*. World Scientific Publishers.

2

Three Important Players of China's Economy

In this chapter I will briefly describe the three important players of China's economy. These are the government, the entrepreneurs and the ordinary citizens and workers.

2.1. The Chinese Government

The Chinese government is organized under the leadership of the Communist Party of China (CPC). The Communist Party exercises leadership by nominating candidates for the most important government positions including the President, who is at the same time Party Secretary, the Premier and Ministers of the State Council which is the executive branch of the government, and the governors of provinces. Furthermore all government organizations including major universities and their departments have Party secretaries who provide leadership and are more powerful than the administrative heads such as university presidents. The principle of party leadership is stated in the Chinese Constitution.

To understand the CPC we have to go back to its founding in 1921 when China was poor, weak and politically divided, much in need of national unity to carry out economic development. The Soviet Union was newly founded after a successful revolution. It had a strong government and a blueprint for rapid economic development. Many patriotic Chinese wanted to follow the Soviet example of a successful revolution, strong government and a concrete plan for economic development. They founded the Communist Party of China following the Soviet model. The Communist Party took over political control and founded the People's Republic of China in 1949 after a long civil war.

From the early 1950s to 1978 China practiced central economic planning modeled after the Soviet Union and economic efficiency was low. Planning was also disrupted by two major political movements initiated by Party Chairman Mao Zedong. The Great Leap Forward Movement of 1958 organized Communes to practice collective farming and led to economic disaster and famine in 1960–1961. Because of the failure of the Great Leap Mao lost political power in the early 1960s. In order to regain power Mao started the Cultural Revolution of 1966 to 1976 by appealing directly to the Chinese youth to attack the party bureaucracy and the established cultural tradition. Urban population were sent to farms to work as laborers. Chinese youths formed Red Guards to take control in the name of Mao and the Cultural Revolution. Children were encouraged to criticize their parents, and students their teachers. Books and cultural treasures were destroyed. Many intellectuals committed suicide.

In September 1976 Mao passed away and Deng Xiaoping soon took over political power as he was able to obtain the support of the Party leadership. The Party needed a drastic change of direction in order to regain the support of the Chinese people. In addition, having learned from experiencing the difficulties and deficiencies of economic planning and observed the successful economic development in the neighboring economies of Hong Kong, Singapore, Taiwan and South Korea, the Party under the leadership of Deng Xiaoping decided to introduce economic reform towards a market oriented economy. Since the leaders do not have a blueprint to guide the reform, they performed experiments to test out possible directions of reform. Over 2000 state-owned enterprises were selected to try out certain autonomy in making production and distribution decisions in the early stage of the reform of state enterprises. Special economic zones were established to experiment with the introduction of foreign investment which had been prohibited. The approach was described as crossing the river by feeling the stones step by step.

Able officials were selected to carry out reform by the Chinese government. Deng selected able leaders like Zhao Ziyang who as Premier in turn had very able ministers in the State Council and very able officials to serve on the State Commission for Reconstructing the Economic System (Economic Reform Commission). I served as adviser of the Commission which had the responsibility to design economic reform to be introduced to the People's Congress for enacting the required new legislation and to the State Council for executive action. The Commission was the most important Commission of the State Council as it was chaired by the Premier himself while previously the most important Commission was the Planning Commission chaired by a Vice Premier, the Planning Commission in the early 1980s being chaired by Yao Yilin, a Vice Premier.

At many meetings with leading members of the Commission I found them to be very pragmatic. Any good institutions of a capitalist economy could be suggested and adopted for China without regard to ideology. They were able. China invited foreign economists to provide suggestions from North America, Japan, Western Europe and even Eastern Europe which was still practicing central planning. The reform officials would be interested in learning about successful economic institutions wherever they might be. They would then decide what institutions would be suitable for China.

China's central government was strong enough to carry out economic reforms. Some government officials were very talented and efficient. I also cooperated with officials of the State Education Commission (elevated from Ministry of Education in 1985 to emphasize the importance of education) to introduce and promote the teaching of modern economics in China when only Marxian economics was taught in the early 1980s. After directing a summer workshop to teach modern economics in Peking University in 1984 and on my way from Shanghai to Hangzhou by train I thought of the idea of selecting top students in China to pursue graduate studies in North America. The Ministry of Education would administer examinations in mathematics and economics (questions in economics were based on my text book, *The Chinese Economy*, Harper & Row, 1985) and I would help place the students to appropriate graduate schools. I sent a telegram to the official in the Ministry of Education suggesting this idea and asking him send his reply to my next stop at Zhongshan University in Guangzhou. When I arrived Zhongshan University three days later I found his reply awaiting and agreeing to my proposal. Examinations were given in the fall of the same year 1984 and I was able to place over 60 students to pursue their PhD degree in North American beginning in the Fall of 1985. Three groups of such students were placed in 1985, 1986 and 1987, making a total of about 160 students. In 1988, the same official in the Ministry of Education (now State Education Commission) decided to introduce a set of core courses to be required in all Universities under its control and the directive was carried out immediately. These instances illustrated the efficiency of economic reform officials.

To carry out economic reform since the early 1980s China was able to select able and dedicated government officials. In addition, the central government is strong and stable enough to carry out important policies. The selection of leaders of the Communist Party who nominate government officials is through indirect elections. Members of Party committees at a lower level beginning with villages and counties elect members at the level above, up to the members of the Central Committee which consists of some 2000 members. Members of the Central Committee elect members of the Political Bureau who in turn elect members of its Standing Committee. The Standing Committee members, now 11 in number, are the most powerful persons in China and they elect the General Secretary who also serves as President of the Chinese government. Political maneuvering aside, this indirect election process enables able people to be elected to lead the Party and the government in China. People may wonder whether a strong dictator like Mao may exist today who will cause instability as during the Great Leap and the Cultural Revolution. The answer is no because Mao was a leader who assumed leadership as a revolutionary leader before the election process of the Party was firmly established. Besides, the Chinese people have learned from the experience of these two political movements and have gained enough economic power as not to accept such disruptions.

The behavior of Chinese government officials has changed, however. In the early stages of reform China was poor and many government officials were eager to introduce changes to achieve rapid economic development, as illustrated by examples from my personal experience cited above. In more recent years after China became richer, there is a tendency for government officials to become more bureaucratic. They desire to hold on to their position and power and are less eager to introduce changes that are risky for fear of losing their position. On the positive side, it is not necessary to adopt large institutional changes since well functioning market institutions are already in place to allow rapid economic development to take place. Many able bureaucrats are ingenious enough to exercise their own initiative to take actions that are beneficial to their own interests and to the development of China. These observations are valid in spite of the wide-spread corruption in China. Corruption affects the distribution of income. It may not adversely affect economic efficiency unless it creates sufficient public discontent to cause substantial political instability that disrupts the functioning of China's market economy. More on corruption in the next section.

The Chinese government takes an active role in the management of the macro-economy, as illustrated by its policy in 2009 to spend some 6 trillion RMB (over 400 billion US dollars) to stimulate the economy during the global economic recession. Western observers have criticized the Chinese government for failure to practice democracy and restriction of freedom of the press. These are not the subject of this chapter. In terms of economic development, China's government has played an important role in introducing economic reform because it is strong, able and pragmatic.

2.2. The Entrepreneurs

While economic reform led by the Chinese government was the major feature of China's economic development for about 25 years since reform started in 1978, economic changes propelled by the Chinese entrepreneurs are the main feature in recent years, as described by chapter 1 of Chow (2010).

The talents and areas of interest of the Chinese entrepreneurs vary, but all are self made and started with very little wealth to begin with. Simply because in the early 1980s all Chinese were poor, potential entrepreneurs started in a level plain field where no one had inherited wealth. This environment is a major factor for selecting the entrepreneurs to succeed mainly on account of their abilities.

To illustrate, several years ago while travelling in Wuxi, I observed the operations of Mr. Tiger's factory producing cigarette lighters that dominated the world market. Mr. Tiger was a worker being laid off by a state-owned enterprise. He started making one or two cigarette lighters a day and later created and managed an enterprise which at the time of my visit was occupying over a quarter of the world market. Another example is Dr. Shi Zhengrong, a PhD in physics who returned to China from Australia in the late 1990s to start a company producing solar panels and was able in five years time to make his company Suntech the second largest producer of solar panels in the world, second only to First Solar in the United States, while he himself became the richest person in China. As a third example, BYD Auto based in Shenzhen, Guangdong Province, was established by founder and President Wang Chuanfu in 2003, sold 448,400 electric cars, and in December 2008 began selling the world's first mass-produced, plug-in hybrid vehicle, the BYD F3DM. In December 2008, Warren Buffet spent $230 million buying up 10% of the stake in the company.

In 2010, Forbes reported that China (excluding Hong Kong which has 25) has 64 billionaires, including 27 new ones (implying an extremely rapid rate of increase), second only to the United States which has 403, or 40 percent of the world total. Based on a list from Forbes, I have found the top six Chinese entrepreneurs whose businesses include beverages, feed, retail, batteries and electric cars and real estate, suggesting that one can succeed in a variety of businesses that provide consumer and producer goods.* Three of the six had a college education while the remaining three did not. I was impressed by the two leading entrepreneurs that I know: Wang Yongching of Taiwan (who passed way three years ago) and Li Karshing of Hong Kong. Both did not have much education and started as low paid workers but had excellent business skill and judgment. Many leading entrepreneurs in mainland China are of the same type.

Entrepreneurship has been developed for thousands of years since the market economy has existed for thousands of years. The Chinese entrepreneurs have their own characteristics, different from the characteristics of entrepreneurs elsewhere, because they are the creation of thousands of years of Chinese history and culture as well as the recent history of turmoil and economic progress. The quality and skill of Chinese entrepreneurs have been inherited from such a long historical tradition. Recent economic turmoil during the Great Leap Forward movement of 1958–1961 and the Cultural Revolution of 1966–1976, as well as the low standard of living during the period of economic planning up to 1978, has taught the recent generation of Chinese the skill to survive and the strong desire to get rich. The recent economic growth shows the younger generation that opportunities are there for them to take. The intelligent entrepreneurs understand the environment and have the instinct and skill to take advantage of it. For example, able Chinese entrepreneurs have taken advantage of the skill and diligence of the workers by motivating them and giving them a sufficiently good set of working conditions as many have done.

2.3. Workers and Ordinary Citizens

The main factor contributing to a nation's ability in achieving economic development is its human capital. Human capital is more important than physical capital, because a well-organized society with

---

*The list can be found in the website http://www.forbes.com/lists/2010/10/billionaires-2010_The-Worlds-Billionaires_CountryOfCitizen_3.html.

able people can always accumulate physical capital. Observe the successful economic development of Germany and Japan which had a shortage of physical capital at the end of World War II, as much physical capital was destroyed by the War. These countries were able to develop rapidly, so were the economies of Hong Kong, Singapore, Taiwan and South Korea, known as four dragons in Asia. China before 1978 also had an abundance of high-quality human capital but the planning system prevented it from functioning properly.

China owes its human capital to its culture and history. In the Shang Dynasty some 4000 years ago, Chinese workers were able to produce the elegant bronze vessels . Market economy was well functioning in the Han dynasty some two thousand years ago, and it was well understood by the great Han historian Sima Qian (Chow, 2007, p. 13). Market economy flourished in the Song Dynasty, 906–1126. It enabled the Chinese economy to develop in the 1920s and 1930s even when there was much political instability and civil war, before the War with Japan beginning in 1937. No wonder after economic reform started the Chinese people were able to develop the economy rapidly from a low starting point.

In discussing human capital, economists have emphasized the role of schooling which is almost equated to education. This concept of human capital is too narrow for the understanding of the role of human capital in economic development. First, years of formal schooling aside, human capital is what one has learned or acquired while growing up and living in a given society. The working habit of the workers and the resourcefulness of the entrepreneurs in China are a part of the Chinese society influenced by its history and cultural tradition. Chinese workers are hard-working. One can even observe this by noting the efficiency of the workers in check-out counters in Chinese supermarkets in the United States. Secondly, family education is as important as formal schooling not only in imparting useful knowledge but also in developing a good habit of learning and a good way of thinking.

For a developing country given its cultural tradition, formal schooling in important in accumulating human capital for economic development. The government can play an important role in promoting formal education, as governments in many countries are doing. Its policy to foster private education at all levels is important. In addition the government can influence the way its citizens think about the value of education. At the same time leading citizens and influential social groups can and should contribute to the education of citizens and the formation of attitude conducive to economic development.

References

Chow, Gregory C. (2007). *China's Economic Transformation*. Blackwell Publishers.

Chow, Gregory C. (2010). *Interpreting China's Economy*. World Scientific.

CHAPTER 3

Is Chinese Capitalism Different?

The rapid economic changes in China have been widely noticed. It is generally agreed that the market institutions in China, however imperfect, have enabled the economy to grow so rapidly. In this essay I try to answer the question, is the Chinese market economy different from other market economies in some essential way?

My answer is positive, as explained in the sections below. Under the assumption that the entrepreneurs are the important driving force to move a market economy forward, the Chinese entrepreneurs behave under a different set of environment as listed below.

3.1. The Chinese Government is Different

3.1.1. *The Chinese government plays a more important role in regulating the economic behavior of the entrepreneurs*

1. The entrepreneurs in establishing a new business and in operating an established business require approval of a set of bureaucrats, of the central government if the enterprise operates nationally or internationally and of the local government where the enterprise is located. Any bureaucrat has an incentive to collect economic rent. Thus the entrepreneurs need to survive this hurdle.

2. Under the dictum that the fittest survives, the entrepreneurs who survive must be fit. To be fit means going through a screening process that selects the talented. I observe that the bureaucrats in China are by

and large intelligent. They are members of the Communist Party which has an indirect election process for selecting more talented people to serve at higher places, although there are also selected through personal favors and connections. The intelligent bureaucrats have an incentive to select the able entrepreneurs to support in order to increase future rents to be collected.

3.1.2. *The Chinese government plays a different role in setting up economic institutions*

China has not experienced similar economic crises during the recent world economic downturn because its institutions are less subject to risks. The financial institutions in China were not allowed to take the kind of risks that American financial institutions could take. The issuers of derivative securities in the US are able to create financial assets, including a stock option, whose values fluctuate greatly without sufficient capital. The financial crisis in the US demonstrates that free exchange can lead to extreme risk taking and economic chaos. The Chinese government is slow in allowing these derivatives to be introduced.

3.2. The Chinese Legal Institutions are Different

It is well recognized that a Western style legal system is not being practiced in China although the Chinese legislature have introduced many laws similar to Western laws to facilitate the conduct of economic activities, especially by foreign investors. These laws are not strictly enforced. To be successful Chinese entrepreneurs have to conduct business in the Chinese way, using Guanxi for example.

3.3. The Chinese Culture is Different

Here I use the term "culture" in a narrow sense. In a broad sense Chinese culture has affected both the behavior of Chinese government and the Chinese legal institutions discussed above. In the narrow sense I refer to the way to conduct business by the entrepreneurs themselves. It is the way they treat their employees and their competitors. And it is the importance of social status in getting things done. It is often said that the US is ruled by law and the Chinese are ruled by people. In China it is who you are that gets things done, often more so than the position that you hold. Deng Xiaoping was the paramount leader of China for years without being the Party Secretary, the highest position in the Chinese political system.

The set of rules implicit from Chinese culture affect the way Chinese entrepreneurs establish their position in society, partly to make his economic activities more successful. In Hong Kong, for example, by contributing large sums to charity, entrepreneurs gain social status which is an important asset in getting things done.

3.4. The Chinese Workers are Different

I do not refer to the abundance of Chinese workers that has led to low wage as an important factor attracting foreign investment. (The relative wage in coastal provinces in China has increased so that some foreign investors have been moving to neighboring countries including India and Vietnam where wages are even lower.) I refer to the working ethics and skill that the Chinese have inherited from thousands of years of market economic activities.

Able Chinese entrepreneurs can take advantage of the skill and diligence of the workers if they are able to motivate them, to give them a sufficiently good working environment as many have done.

Given that the Chinese entrepreneurs are working under different set of environmental conditions their behavior will be different according to economic theory. Maximization subject to a different set of constraints will in general lead to different economic behavior. We then have to discuss how their behavior is different from that of entrepreneurs in other market economies.

CHAPTER 4

Economic Planning in China

This paper provides an up-to-date study of economic planning in China as it affects the economic development, growth and fluctuations of the Chinese economy. Although economic planning has been practiced in China since 1953 when the first Five-Year Plan began, its nature has changed after economic reform started in 1978. Market reform reduced the importance of central planning, but more recently the global economic recession and China's active macro-economic policy interventions have increased the importance of economic planning.

Our discussion is divided into the following sections: 1. Role of planning in the Chinese economy. 2. Scope of planning. 3. Numerical targets of the Plan and the degree to which the targets are met. 4. Organization of the NDRC. 5. How a plan is implemented. 6. Effects of planning on China's economic development.

4.1. Role of Planning in the Chinese Economy

The Chinese economy is a mixed economy as it combines important features of a market economy and a planned economy. To understand the role of economic planning in China it is necessary to review its history briefly. During the period from 1953 when the first Five-Year Plan began to the end of the 1970s, China practiced central planning under the direction of the State Planning Commission (SPC). The main function of planning was to direct the production of major products by state-owned enterprises. The State Council had a large number of ministries, most of which were responsible for the production of the corresponding products. There were ministries for agriculture and fisheries, forestry, coal, petroleum, chemical products, metallurgy, consumer products, textile, machine building, electronics, nuclear energy, aircraft, ammunitions, space, geology and mineral resources, water resources and electric power, railroads, transportation and communications, posts and telecommunications, urban and rural construction and environmental protection, finance, commerce, etc.

Beginning in 1978 the Chinese government changed the economic system gradually towards a market economy, allowing non-state enterprises to produce and compete with state enterprises. The Commission for Restructuring the Economic System was established in 1982 to direct economic reform. This Commission was under the chairmanship of the Prime Minister himself, while the Planning Commission was chaired by a Vice Premier. In 1998, the SPC was renamed as the State Development Planning Commission (SDPC), which then merged with the Commission for Restructuring the Economic System and the State Economic and Trade Commission (SETC). In 2006 it was renamed as the National Development and Reform Commission (NDRC), with the term "planning" omitted perhaps to convey to the world that China was no longer a centrally planned economy. The NDRC continues to prepare Five-Year Plans based on a draft from the Central Committee of the Communist Party. Each plan has to be approved by the National People's Congress.

From the above brief description of the historical development of the NDRC, we note that historical tradition affects the nature and functioning of economic planning in China today. Many of the departments, bureaus and officers in the component predecessor commissions remain as well as the thinking and working habit of the staffs within these organizations. During the period of economic reform beginning in 1978, Chinese government officials were shown the efficacy of the market economy by experimentation but they continued to believe in the importance of planning. The course of economic reform was to allow elements of both the market economy and economic planning to coexist and serve the Chinese economy. State and non-state enterprises coexist and compete with one another. Although a market economy functions effectively in China, the idea that planning is essential for China's economic development remains in the mind of government officials until today.

4.2. Scope of Planning

The scope of planning today can be described by the contents of the most recent two Five-Year Plans. I will use the main parts of the 12th Five-Year Plan (from 2011–2015) as the basis and indicate the parts of the 11th Five-Year Plan which are in common or different. The 16 parts of the 12th Five-Year Plan are as follows:

1. Guiding principles and general directions, as specified in Chapters 1 to 4.
2. Agriculture (same for 11th Five-Year Plan).
3. Upgrading industry (same).
4. Promoting the service sector (same).
5. Regional and urban development (same).
6. Energy and environment (same).
7. Education, science and technology (same).
8. People's livelihood and welfare (new).
9. Strengthening management of society (new).
10. Promoting socialist culture (same, in part 12).
11. Perfecting economic Reform (same, in part 8).
12. Advancing the open door policy (same, in part 9).
13. Promoting democracy under socialism (same, in part 11).
14. Establishing a harmonious society (same, in part 10).
15. Strengthening defense (same, in part 13).
16. Plan execution (same, in part 14).

From the 16 parts we note four areas covered by the work of the National Development and Reform Commission. The first is the work carried out by the former State Planning Commission, namely, production in different sectors as specified by parts 2 to 7. The second is the work of the former Commission for Restructuring the Economic System, including parts 11 and 12. The third is social stability and welfare, including parts 8, 9, 10, 13 and 14. The fourth area is defense, part 15. As a result of economic reform in part 11, government institutions such as a modern central bank was set up to conduct monetary policy for a market economy. This is not strictly speaking a part of planning although it is a part of the work of NDRC.

By comparing the two Five-Year Plans we note that the 12th Five-Year Plan has added two new parts to the 11th Five-Year Plan. The new parts are 8, People's livelihood and welfare and 9, Strengthening management of society. These new parts suggest that there is an increase in the concern on the part of the Communist Party and the Chinese government with the livelihood and welfare of the people, and with the stability of the society. The latter may be due to the increasing complexity in managing the society in the course of rapid economic development. The complexity has resulted partly from the global recession beginning in 2008 and partly from the recent political instability in the Middle East and North Africa.

Among the new directions of the 12th Five-Year Plan the following should be noted. Partly to achieve the new goals set in parts 8 and 9, the 12th Five-Year Plan aims to promote the expansion of aggregate consumption as a fraction of GDP while building the social security net. In achieving the traditional goals it will increase government expenditures to build mass infrastructure, to reduce income disparity and regional differences and to make greater investment in human capital via higher education and R&D.

4.3. Numerical Targets and the Degree to Which They are Met

I present in Table 1 a selected set of numerical targets of the 11th Five-Year Plan and the extent to which they were met as reported in official government statistics.

This table provides some of the important targets specified by a Five-Year Plan. It also shows that the targets are set in such a way that most can be met. Of the 17 targets included in the table, all except four have been exceeded by the realized amount (marked by E in the

Table 1.   The 11th Five-Year Plan Targets and Realizations.

	2005	Target 2010	Target increase	Realized 2010	Realized increase
GDP (trillion)	18.5		7.5%/year	39.8	11.2%/year E
Per capita GDP	14,185		6.6%/year	29748	10.6%/year E
Increase in service sector (% of output)	40.5%		3%	43.0%	2.5% N
Increase in service employment (% of total)	31.3%		4%	34.8%	3.5% N
Expenditure on research (% of GDP)	1.3%	2%	0.7%	1.75%	0.45% N
Urbanization rate	43%	47%	4%	47.5%	4.5% E
Population (10,000)	130,756	136,000	<8‰	134,100	5.1‰
Reduction in energy use			20%		19.1% N
Cultivated land (100 million hecters)	1.22	1.2	−0.3%/year	1.212	−0.13%/year E
Carbon emission reduction			10%/year		14.29%/year E
Years of schooling (mean for population)	8.5	9	0.5%/year	9	0.5%/year E
Urban retirement insurance coverage (100 million)	1.74	2.23	5.1%/year	2.57	8.1%/year E
Rural health insurance coverage	23.5%	>80%	>56.5%/year	96.3%	>72.8%/year E
Increase in urban employment (10,000)			4500		5771 E
Urban unemployment rate	4.2%	5%		4.1%	E
Urban disposable income per capita (Yuan)	10,493		5%/year	19109	9.7%/year E
Rural net income per capita (Yuan)	3255		5%/year	5919	8.9%/year E

Note: E for exceeding target; N for not exceeding.

last column of the table). The four are the output of the service sector as a percentage of total output, employment in the service sectors as a percentage of total employment, expenditure on research as a percentage of GDP and the percentage reduction in the use of energy (marked by N in the last column of the table). The realization of total population is not classified, because one can question whether a realization of a larger population than the target is desirable or not. In any case the realized figure is within the range targeted. Setting most targets that can be met has been a practice not only of the 11th and 12th Five-Year Plan but in other Five-Year Plans of recent years also. The targets serve to call the attention of the Chinese people and government officials involved to the specific economic objectives and to rally their support to achieve them.

4.4. Organization of the NDRC

To understand how the NDRC carries out its tasks let us look at its organization chart to find out how the responsibilities are divided. The chart shows a large number of departments, bureaus and officers which were inherited from the previous parent Commissions and not designed rationally to perform the tasks of the present Commission.

According to the official website of the National Development and Reform Commission, its functional departments/bureaus/offices include:

- General Office
- Office of Policy Studies
- Department of Development Planning
- Department of National Economy
- Bureau of Economic Operations (Inter-Ministerial Office of the Alleviation of Enterprise Burden under the State Council)
- Department of Economic System Reform
- Department of Fixed Assets Investment
- Department of Industrial Policies

- Department of Foreign Capital Utilization
- Department of Regional Economy
- Department of Rural Economy
- Department of Industry (Office of Rare Earth, Office of Salt Industry Administration, National Chemical Weapons Convention Implementation Office)
- Department of High-Tech Industry
- Department of Resource Conservation and Environmental Protection
- Department of National Coordination Committee for Climate a new entry Change
- Department of Social Development
- Department of Trade
- Department of Fiscal and Financial Affairs
- Department of Price
- Department of Price Supervision
- Department of Employment and Income Distribution
- Department of Laws and Regulations
- Department of International Cooperation
- Department of Personnel
- Office of National Economic Mobilization
- Office of Key Project Inspectors
- Office of the Leading Group for Western Region Development of the State Council
- Office of the Leading Group for Revitalizing Northeast China and Other Old Industrial Bases of the State Council

This list shows that the organization of NDRC is the result of its historical development and not of rational design for the purpose of achieving its current important tasks. However, such a horizontal design can serve the objective of NDRC because it is essentially a staff and not line organization. Its task is to set the targets of planning while leaving the responsibility of plan execution to the ministries and officers of the State Council. The NDRC is where the actions are planned and not where the plan is executed.

4.5. How is the Planning Carried Out?

It is mainly the ministries and offices of the State Council that carry out the plan drafted by the various departments, bureaus and offices of the NDRC. Because the Chinese government has substantial amounts of economic resources under its direct control through the ownership of shares of industrial and commercial enterprises it can achieve the objectives set out by the Five-Year Plan by using these resources. It can also use fiscal and monetary policies to influence the use of resources controlled by non-government economic units. Thus we can classify the means to achieve the planning objectives into two categories.

1. Using resources under the direct control of the government (as in a socialist economy) by directing state-owned enterprises and government agencies to produce specific kinds of goods and services. Besides, the Chinese government has direct control over the citizens in their economic behavior and can order the citizens to achieve targets of the Plan. A notable example is the control of the birth rate under the one-child per family policy. This policy has been modified to allow two children for families with both parents being a single child and to allow the payment of fines for an extra child.

2. Influencing the activities of economic agents in the private sector

a. Use government expenditures to obtain the work by private economic organizations. Contract out government projects.
b. Use economic incentives to influence the work of non-government economic organizations, including tax and subsidies in fiscal policies and setting interest rates and money supply as in monetary policies.

In reality production of many sectors of the Chinese economy are carried out by both state-owned and non-state enterprises. This is because the Chinese government is pragmatic in allowing both sets of enterprises to compete in order to increase economic efficiency.

Politically, China is under the leadership of the Communist Party. As the NDRC received directions from the Party in drafting the Five-Year Plan, the Party exercises its power by directing the Party secretaries in all the units having responsibilities in carrying out all aspects of the Plan. On the part of the government, the chain of command goes from the central government to governments at the provincial, city, county and village levels, for the purpose of economic planning and other activities as well. Government actions at all levels are under the direction of the Party at the corresponding level as just pointed out.

4.6. Effects of Planning on China's Economic Development

How does the planning system affect the functioning of the Chinese economy? Planning symbolizes the tradition of collectivism of the Chinese society, in contrast with individualism in the United States. The Chinese government sets out a five-year plan to get the support not only of government officials but of all Chinese people outside the government to help achieve the tasks specified by the Plan. Even though some of the targets set out in the Plan are not met in practice, the Chinese people are urged to do their part as detailed in the different parts of the Plan. For an observer, knowledge of the Plan provides the areas of economic activities where the government is paying attention. The United States does not have such a planning system. There is no need to watch such a government plan to understand the development of the US economy. The planning system in China helps define the "mixed economy" for China.

To conclude this paper I summarize two important reasons why understanding economic planning in China is important.

1. Domestically, we need to understand the four areas of government activities affecting the economy: (1) directing output of individual industrial sectors and regions, (2) continuing reform of the market institutions and the open door policies, (3) caring for social welfare and social stability and (4) defense. The activities in the first three are much more extensive than in the US. We see the contrast between

collectivism in China vs. individual freedom in the US, between strong government vs. limited government in the US, and between a fairly effective government vs. a somewhat divided government in the US. However, having such a planning system does not imply that China is free of serious economic problems such as wastes, inflation and social instability generated by income inequality that need to be resolved.

2. Internationally, we can better understand the nature of economic cooperation and competition between the two groups of nations, one led by the US that advocates the "Washington Consensus" to promote free trade and globalization, and the second led by China that limits the excesses of free markets and practices government directions of economic activities. This paper describes the internal forces at work to achieve China's global agenda. Even though the planning system has deficiencies in China's mixed economy, it is an asset more than a liability for China to play its role as a leader of the world economy.

CHAPTER 5

Role of Economists in China's Economic Development*

Today I am delighted to speak to you on a topic of mutual interest: the role of economists in China's economic development. I will speak about the role of economists in China's government, in academic institutions and in business enterprises, and suggest ways to make the work of economists more effective. Finally I will point out what the Chinese Economists Society can do to promote the contributions of economists in China's economic development.

5.1. Role in the Government

Economists are important in China's government for three reasons. First is the historical tradition of respect for scholars. Scholars served as government officials throughout Chinese history. Second is the important contributions that economists have made in recent years of rapid economic development. The third is the practice of economic planning today that requires the talents of economists.

Important contributions of economists in recent years include working in the Commission for Reconstructing the Economic System which was established in 1982 to introduce market institutions required for the efficient functioning of China's market economy. It

---

*An invited address before the annual meeting of the Chinese Economists Society in Beijing on June 18, 2011.

also includes working in the National People's Congress to draft new legislation needed for a market economy. Examples are the Central Bank Law of 1995 serving as the basis for the conduct of monetary policy and the Commercial Bank Law of 1995 serving as the basis for the functioning of banking and financial institutions. Economists also work in the news media, appear on the television programs and write important newspaper articles as these institutions are operated by the Chinese government.

On the subject of economic planning the National Development and Reform Commission (NDRC) has taken over functions from the previous State Planning Commission, the Commission for Restructuring the Economic System and the State Economic Commission. It continues to draft Five-Year Plans to guide the economic development of China. Economists serve in the NDRC, in the People's Bank which carries out monetary policy and in different ministries and offices of the State Council, not to speak of posts in provincial, city and local governments. Besides having academic training these economists have learned from experience in their posts to make policy decisions for the development and management of the economy.

In the 1980s I served as an adviser to the Commission for Restructuring the Economic System and found its leading members to be very able and open-minded. Economists and policy makers can learn from one another if they are willing to keep an open mind and consider seriously opposite viewpoints as they did in deliberations of the Commission for Restructuring the Economic System. Today when major decisions are made, such as whether to revalue the RMB or to introduce more restrictive monetary policies, there are bound to be disagreements among policy makers and among economists. Both the policy makers and the economists as advisers will do well by keeping an open mind. While trying to present one's own viewpoint as well as one can, an economist should be willing to change his mind if there are convincing arguments favoring an opposite viewpoint. This attitude on the part of all participants will enable a wiser decision to be made.

Today there are two opposing forces at work that affect the quality of economic deliberations in government decision making. On the positive side, the economists in China are better trained than before.

On the negative side, as China has become richer, government officials are concerned with protecting their positions and less eager to accept new ideas for fear of rocking the boat. Such attitude is hampering the economic development of China.

5.2. Role in Academic and Research Institutions

The field of economics is young in China, having been developed only since the mid-1980s, but the progress of economic teaching and research has been rapid. The quality of economic journals published in China has improved. A research economist can choose his field of research according to his own interest, be it the forefront of research as defined by publications in world-class academic journals or more applied research including empirical studies of the Chinese economy. Chinese economists can be expected to do outstanding research that will be recognized world wide in the future, partly because the working of the Chinese economy itself provides excellent topics to stimulate research in China. Creative research ideas are stimulated by problems in the environment in which the researchers live. For example, Keynes' *General Theory* and Friedman's free market ideas were both stimulated by economic problems and conditions of the time.

Teaching in the leading schools of economics has improved. Encouraging signs are seen in some leading schools of economics in China as they are importing well trained economists at different levels from abroad and introducing innovative ideas for teaching and research. Although absorbing these economists into the existing faculty have created administrative problems which are being resolved. The net effect of these developments is positive for upgrading economics education in China. The influence of the top schools is spreading. We may see the beginning of a golden period of teaching and research in China in economics and in other fields as well.

Yet the cooperation among the leading schools of economics can be improved. In the US, while the top universities compete with one another they also take advantage of the strengths of their competitors and try to learn from them. For example, there is a regular conference of econometricians in seven universities in the US East Coast from Yale, Columbia, New York University to Princeton University and the University of Pennsylvania that meets regularly with one group serving as host. Papers are presented and discussed at each conference. There are a number of outstanding schools of economics or management in Beijing and in Shanghai. These schools can easily initiate regular seminars as do Harvard and MIT in Cambridge MA.

Cooperation among economic institutions is consistent with the Chinese tradition of letting one hundred flowers bloom. During the golden Spring and Autumn period for China's intellectual development, leaders of different schools of thought were advancing their own ideas but they respected one another and learned from one another. Confucius paid his due respect to Lao Zi. To let one hundred flowers bloom we need to make the faculties of economics international. In American universities faculty members have come from many nations. Chinese universities should be open to scholars from all over the world and welcome the best to teach and do research.

If the Chinese government encourages overseas Chinese scholars to return to work in China and if Chinese schools of economics actively recruit fresh Chinese PhDs from the US, why not invite foreign scholars to serve in Chinese universities also? This will strengthen their faculties and advance the process of globalization for China. In academic discussions it is meaningless to argue whether advanced mathematics should be used. Different economists should be free to choose their tools to fit the problem at hand.

Economics teaching and research can be developed from the bottom up. Economic reform in China has allowed autonomy for state-owned enterprises and competition from private enterprises but has not given sufficient autonomy to major universities. China's universities are still tightly controlled by the Chinese government. To improve economics education in Chinese universities, one possibility is enlightened leadership from above and another is innovations from below. There are leaders in individual schools of economics in China today who on their own find innovative ways for administering, teaching and research in order to improve their own schools. One example is the hiring of a distinguished foreign scholar to be Dean of a school of economics. Such decentralized effort will spread and help improve China's economics education and research.

5.3. Role in Business Enterprises

Economic thinking is important for the making of wise decisions in business. Knowledge of macro economics provides an understanding of the environment in which a firm operates. Knowledge of micro economics provides an understanding of the competitive environment and suggests ways to deal with one's competitors. Furthermore, economic thinking is a type of analytical thinking that is useful for decision making. Analytical skills in solving economic problems are applicable to solving business problems as well. Decision-making under uncertainty is an important part of the subject of economics. It is useful for dealing with situations involving risk taking in business. How such economic thinking can be effectively applied in business decisions is learned by practice. Economists working in business have opportunities to learn such skills on the job. Chinese economists working in business enterprises are learning such skills as are economists in other countries.

In China, although the private sector has contributed more than the government sector in the production of total output of goods and services, economists have played a less important role in private enterprises. The most innovative entrepreneurs in China are not economists and some are not even highly educated. Many successful enterprises do not hire economists in important posts.

Today EMBA programs have become very popular in China in filling the need of economics education for top executives. Many such programs are international, jointly operated with a foreign business school. As the technology level of Chinese enterprises rises, successful entrepreneurs will be more educated and professional economists will become more important because economic thinking is useful for decision making in business.

5.4. Role of the Chinese Economists Society

CES is playing an important role in China's economic development by fostering the interchange of ideas among Chinese economists and promoting the field of economics in general.

If the organizers and participants of future CES, conferences will consider the role that economists can play in China's economic development as an important topic and devote sessions and individual papers relevant to this topic, CES can contribute further to the development of the Chinese economy.

Free to Choose in China*

What have been the significant changes in China's economic and political institutions? I will answer this question by discussing eight topics from Milton and Rose Friedman's book *Free to Choose*. The topics are economic freedom, the relation between economic and political freedom, the role of government, social welfare, education, consumer protection, macroeconomic policy and trends in the development of economic and political freedom.

6.1. Economic Freedom in the Last Half Century

There have been significant changes in economic freedom in China in the last half century. Economic freedom began to be severely restricted when central planning was introduced in 1953. It has been increased steadily since economic reform started in 1978. Today there is much economic freedom in China.

The Chinese government adopted Soviet-style central economic planning in 1953 when it initiated the first Five-Year Plan of 1953–1957. For a quarter of a century that followed, freedom in production, distribution and consumption was restricted. For industrial production private enterprises were converted into state-owned enterprises which had to fulfill output targets approved by central

---

*Published in *The Legacy of Milton and Rose Friedman's Free to Choose*, edited by Mark A. Wayne, Harvey Rosenblum and Robert L. Formaini. Dullas, Texas: Federal Reserve Bank of Dallas, 2004, pp. 153–171.

planning. Materials used in production were centrally allocated. Urban workers were assigned jobs in the state-enterprises and could not move from city to city.

In agriculture, the Commune system was established in 1958. Private farming was abolished. The farmers in a traditional village were organized as a team in a Commune to farm collectively. Free trade of farm products was abolished. Rural markets were banned. Each team in a Commune was assigned quotas of output to be delivered to a government procurement agency for distribution in urban areas. A system of rationing of consumer goods in urban areas was put in place. Each consumer was given coupons to buy specified amounts of food, grain, oil, eggs and cloth. Retail stores were operated by the government. There was no free market for housing. Housing units were assigned to employees by their work units at very low rents. Privately automobiles were non-existent.

China's door was closed to the outside world. Foreign trade was handled by the government which determined the exports and imports of specific products to and from specific countries. The main trading partners were the Soviet bloc countries. Foreign investment from Western countries was not welcome. Chinese citizens were not allowed to travel abroad. The border with Hong Kong which had been opened without any restrictions was closed in the early 1950s.

Recognizing the shortcomings of central economic planning from years of experience and witnessing the economic success of neighboring market economies of Hong Kong, Singapore, Taiwan and South Korea, the Chinese government under the leadership of Deng Xiaoping began economic reform towards a market-oriented economy in 1978. In agriculture, private farming was revived. The Commune system was abolished by 1982. This change occurred through initiatives from below when some commune leaders discovered that output quotas could be met by assigning a piece of land to each farm household to farm and collecting a quota of output from it, rather than by having all farm households in a team to farm collectively. Under this "household responsibility system" output increased significantly because the farmers could reap the fruits of their additional effort. The central government soon adopted this system as national policy. Increase in farm output allowed the gradual abandonment of the rationing of consumer goods.

Urban industrial reform took several steps that were introduced in a period of about two decades, from granting autonomy to state enterprises in production decisions to converting them to share-holding corporations traded in stock markets in the late 1990s. China's door was opened to foreign trade and investment. In 2001 China joined the World Trade Organization to open its door further by lowering tariffs and allowing more foreign competition in agriculture, manufacturing and service industries and in domestic trade. Observers attribute the success of China's economic reform to the gradual and experimental approach taken by the leaders who were pragmatic and adopted what worked without being subject to ideological constraints. As Deng advised, "Seek truth from facts."

Today China has a well-functioning market economy in spite of its shortcomings. Economic freedom of the citizens has been greatly enhanced. Private enterprises have flourished. Rationing has been abolished since the early 1980s and consumer goods are abundant in supply. Housing has been privatized. The demand for new automobiles in 2003 is to exceed 4.2 million units. The Chinese people can travel freely both inside and outside the country, many having come to the United States to study. They can choose and change their jobs fairly freely, although many do not move because of the benefits of entitlements under the welfare system administered by state-owned enterprises.

There are unions but there is no union power that restricts the freedom of employers to choose workers and the freedom of non-union workers to choose their jobs. There appears to be no serious infringement of economic freedom in China, with the exception of the one-child policy that allows only one child for an urban family and an additional child for a rural family if the first child is a girl.

6.2. Relation of Economic Freedom and Political Freedom

On pages 2–3 of *Free to Choose* we read: "Economic Freedom is an essential requisite for political freedom. By enabling people to cooperate with one another without coercion or central direction, it reduces the area over which political power is exercised. In addition, by dispersion of power, the free market provides an offset to whatever concentration of political power may arise." China provides many examples for these observations.

As private farming under the household responsibility system replaced collective farming under the Commune System, agricultural output increased in the early 1980s and labor was free to move. In a trip along the Yangtze to see the Three Gorges in 1982, I witnessed many farmers on the boat carrying farm products to neighboring areas for sale and carpenter tools to find work elsewhere. As economic freedom increased, the administration of the Commune system ceased to function.

There remained the need to provide security, to protect public land and to attend to the public affairs of rural villages that were formerly within the domain of the Commune system. This was a primary reason for the direct elections of village officials that have become widespread in rural China. The central government endorses such elections because the elected officials performed important functions in Chinese villages. Village elections in China are a major component of the change of China's political institutions toward a more democratic government.

As more consumer goods became available, rationing was no longer necessary. Goods began to be distributed in rural markets and in collectively or privately owned stores in urban areas. The role of government procurement and trading is greatly reduced. Services formerly provided by employees in government-owned retail stores, hotels, train stations, theatres and other service-providing establishments are now provided by private enterprises for profit. The quality of services has greatly improved. The sphere of government influence has been reduced in all respects of economic life, including production, distribution, employment, foreign trade and foreign investment. Government bureaucrats are replaced by non-government employees who are more service minded. All this "reduces the area over which political power is exercised."

The wide-spread abuse of economic power under the previous system of government ownership of assets and government control of resource allocation has been reduced with the rise of the free market. The system of economic planning itself induced the Chinese to take full advantage of the assets under their control. Under the system of central planning major economic assets were owned and controlled by the government, but in reality the government had to assign people to control and use the assets on its behalf and in the name of the state. The people who had the power to manage government assets used them for their own benefits. Corruption was only one example when the bureaucrats controlling some economic assets extracted money from people who desired to use them. A driver of a government owned car could use the car for personal benefits. If another person desired to use the car he would have to compensate or appease the driver since there were no taxi cabs available.

Under this system the Chinese people became frustrated when they had to beg to get served or to acquire the essential consumer goods. They then aired their frustrations and returned the favor to others when other people desired goods and services from them. The quality of services provided in China was poor in general. People were unkind to one another whenever one person needed something from someone who had control of the needed asset or service. Barters became widespread. A person in charge of selling low-price and scarce theatre tickets could exchange the tickets for scarce consumer goods distributed in government stores.

With the appearance of the market economy, the quality of services provided by the Chinese people has gradually improved, and the people have been kinder to one another. Now money can be used to purchase goods and services. Fewer people connected with the government have monopoly power over the control of economic resources that others need.

As collective and private enterprises flourished, a group of well-to-do citizens have emerged and gained influence and economic power in the Chinese society. In the late 1990s, under the leadership of General Secretary Jiang Zemin the Chinese Communist Party began to accept capitalists to its membership. China has a one-party system. There are other political parties but none can control the Chinese government. They exercise their political influence mainly through a

National Political Consultative Conference which represents diverse political interests and meets regularly at the same time as the National People's Congress. The recommendations of the Conference are seriously considered by the People's Congress. Political power of the people is exercised by indirect elections of members of the People's Congress and of the members of the Central Committee of the Communist Party, the latter by members of the Party members only. To the extent that membership of the Communist Party is more open, more people will have more political freedom and more opportunities to participate in government affairs.

As economic freedom has increased, so has political freedom although it is difficult to ascertain the precise effect of the former on the latter. Political freedom is in principle guaranteed in the Chinese Constitution adopted by the People's Congress on December 4, 1982. In Chapter I, "General Principles," Article 2 states, "All power in the PRC belongs to the people. The organs through which the people exercise state power are the National People's Congress and the local people's congresses at different levels." Article 28 states, "The state maintains public order and suppresses treasonable and other counter-revolutionary activities; it penalizes actions that endanger public security and disrupt the socialist economy ..." In Chapter II, "The Fundamental Rights and Duties of Citizens," Article 35 provides all citizens "freedom of speech, the press, of assembly, of association, of procession and demonstration" while Article 36 provides "freedom of religious belief." However, the stated freedoms can be restricted by appealing to Article 28 of the Constitution.

In reality the Chinese people do have much more freedom than before. They can talk freely in private gatherings and even openly in professional meetings without fear of being prosecuted. For instance, a Chinese economics professor openly criticized the labor theory of value in Marxian economics in a paper presented before a conference in Beijing in 1999. There is freedom of the press to a considerable extent as the non-government press has expanded rapidly in recent years and attracted a large readership. This includes daily or weekly newspapers, magazines and books. Opinions expressed therein are open and free, subject to only a minor degree of censorship. Censorship of foreign books is almost non-existent.

Information available to the public is somewhat restricted because the government has control over TV and radio stations as well as the Internet. However, the control is limited because the Chinese have access to short-wave radios and it is difficult to control the use of fax machines and the flow of information through the Internet. People residing near Hong Kong can get access to TV stations in Hong Kong which are mainly private and free.

Religious freedom has increased as illustrated by the rapid increase in attendance in Christian churches and worship in Buddhist temples. Church attendance has been affected by the efforts of overseas Chinese, especially those in Hong Kong, who invest in China's economic and educational institutions and sometimes also engage in religious activities.

Government control of the press has been reduced partly because citizen-initiated newspaper has increased in response to the increase in demand for reading material in an affluent society. Demand for officially printed material has declined. As the August 5, 2003 issue of *People's Daily* reports, "Party and government-run newspapers and magazines will be forced to commercialize or face closure under major reforms... National Bureau of Statistics show that there were 2,137 newspapers in China last year, but newspapers relying on administrative orders for subscribers accounted for 40% of the total." Government and Party organizations were asked to close their newspapers or magazines if they do not have sufficient paying subscribers.

Under a one-party political system which limits political freedom, there is much economic freedom in China for political freedom is not a necessary condition for economic freedom. Economic freedom will help increase political freedom but political freedom may not help increase, and can sometimes reduce, economic freedom as illustrated by many examples in the United States that have been documented in *Free To Choose*. There is much political freedom in the United States, but many infringements of economic freedom are the subject of *Free to Choose*.

6.3. The Role of Government

On page 5 of *Free To Choose*, we read: "The view that government's role is to serve as an umpire to prevent individuals from coercing one another was replaced by the view that government's role is to serve as a parent charged with the duty of coercing some to aid others."

China's experience illustrates very well "the government's [proper] role as an umpire to prevent individuals from coercing one another." In China, the need for the government to provide law and order is very important, because law and order is important for social stability and economic progress.

As someone accustomed to law and order in the United States since 1948, it has taken me several visits to China to appreciate its importance. Several experiences impressed me. In 1982 when I tried to send a telegram in a post office in Guangzhou, I found that people did not line up in front of the service window and there was no way for me to get to the front to submit the draft of my telegram. I had to let a Chinese friend fight his way through to send the telegram. I wished an officer had been there to guide people to line up.

As a second experience, my wife and I were provided a tour guide while visiting Confucius' Temple in Shandong province in 1985. As the guide was explaining the points of interest to us, people began to crowd in and surrounded the guide to the point that Paula and I were so far separated from him that we could not hear what he was saying. As a third example, I was traveling by car to visit the site of Yuan Ming Yuan in Beijing. As we approached the site, we found a road block set up illegally by local residents to collect tolls. Our driver had to pay the toll before he could drive through. Extraction of fees of all kinds by local residents from travelers passing through their territories was and is quite common in China. A strong government is needed to prevent some citizens from extracting rents illegally from others.

The Chinese government has been urged to protect intellectual property rights which are violated in China in the sale of pirated CDs of computer software, music and movies. Many Chinese regard law and order more important than freedom, and desire a strong government to protect them from coercion by others.

The second and improper role of the government — "to serve as a parent charged with the duty of coercing some to aid others" — can be illustrated by many examples in the early years of the People's Republic of China (PRC). Private land was redistributed in the early 1950s to the farmers. Private enterprises were turned to state-owned enterprises. Output of farmers produced in the Communes were taxed for distribution to the urban population. Such coercions have been reduced with the introduction of market institutions where private property is respected. At the same time the growing importance of the first, legitimate role of the government — "as an umpire to prevent individuals from coercing one another" — signifies that the political system in China has improved.

6.4. Social Welfare

During the period of central planning, job security was guaranteed and support for the aged was provided by the Communes in rural areas and by the state-owned enterprises and other government institutions to their employees in the urban areas. Health care in the entire country was provided under an efficient three-tier system, with village doctors treating simple illnesses in village stations, physicians with three years of medical training after high school in health centers and better trained doctors in city hospitals in turn taking care of more difficult illnesses. A community financed "Cooperative Medical System" (CMS) funded and organized health care for almost the entire rural population. Health centers and hospitals associated with state-owned enterprises and other government institutions cared for the employees and their family members.

With the introduction of economic reform the Commune system broke down and state-owned enterprises were made financially independent and downsized. Private farmers had to find their own work and support themselves at old age. Urban workers can become unemployed. In rural areas, agricultural reforms in the early 1980s led to the disintegration of the cooperative organizations that formed the basis of CMS. The rural population had to finance their own health care while many village doctors had their own private practice. In the urban area, state enterprises and other government organizations had difficulty in financing the health care of their employees.

Since the mid-1990s, the Chinese government has attempted to set up step by step a nationally unified social security system for the urban population, under the central management of the labor and social security administration departments and with social insurance funds partly contributed by the central government. Labor and social security departments at all levels are responsible for the collection, management and payment of the social insurance funds. Besides contributions from employers and employees as stated below the central government allocated 98.2 billion yuan in 2001 for social security payments, 5.18 times the amount in 1998 as it was expanding the system to cover larger segments of the population in steps.[†]

In 1997, a uniform basic old-age insurance system for enterprise employees was established, financed by 20% of the enterprise wage bill and 8% of the employee's wage. A part of the premiums from enterprises go to mutual assistance funds and the rest to personal accounts while the premiums from the employees go entirely to personal accounts that belong to the employees themselves and can be inherited. Employees participating in this program increased from 86.71 million in late 1997 to 108.02 million at the end of 2001 while the number receiving pensions increased from 25.33 million to 33.81 million, with the average monthly basic pension per person increasing from 430 yuan to 556 yuan. The rural population pay their own insurance premiums and withdraw funds from personal accounts with subsidies from the government.

In 1999, an unemployment insurance system was introduced, financed by 2% of the wage bill paid by employers and 1% paid by employees. Unemployment insurance benefits are lower than the minimum wage but higher than the minimum living allowance guaranteed for all laid-off workers. The period of drawing insurance depends on

---

[†]All statistics on the development of the social security system can be found in the website of the *People's Daily*, http://english.peopledaily.com.cn/, under "White Paper on Labor and Social Security in China" in the section "White Papers of Chinese Government."

the length of the period in which insurance payments have been paid, with 24 months as the maximum. The number of persons insured increased from 79.28 million in 1998 to 103.55 million in 2001.

On health care, important policies were announced on January 15, 1997 in the "Decision on Health Reform and Development by the Central Party Committee and State Council." The basic objective of the Decision is to insure that every Chinese will have access to basic health protection. For the rural population the strategy is to develop and improve CMS through education, by mobilizing more farmers to participate and gradually expanding its coverage. In 1998, a basic medical insurance system for urban employees was established, financed by 6% of the wage bill of employing units and 2% of the personal wages. By the end of 2001, 76.29 million employees had participated in basic insurance programs. In addition, free medical services and other forms of health care systems covered over 100 million urban population.

In terms of saving for old age, the rural population in China has more freedom than the urban population to make their decisions but are subject to more risks. The urban population has their own personal accounts with amounts depending on their own contributions. Their old age insurance system has features similar to the pension system in American universities, with both the employer and employee contributing to the fund and with each employee having his personal account. The rural population in China have more freedom to choose their work but are not guaranteed unemployment benefits as are the urban workers. In terms of health care, the Chinese government has a policy to provide basic care for the entire population.

6.5. Education

In China the government has controlled the education system since the early 1950s, but in recent years the role of non-government operated and financed education at all levels has become very important.

When the government decided to adopt Soviet-type economic planning in the early 1950s, the system of higher education was modeled after the Soviet Union along with economic planning. The government seized control of all educational institutions. Private universities were closed and converted into public educational institutions. Liberal education ceased to exist. Education served mainly the purpose of economic development. For this purpose it was believed that a university student should concentrate on one subject, rather than receiving a general liberal education, and that each university should specialize also. Former universities, public and private, were reorganized. One university was divided into several more specialized institutions. The school of arts and sciences, the medical school, the engineering school, and the school of agriculture of one university were separated and became colleges on their own. Each government ministry responsible for the production and distribution of one major product had under its control colleges to train people to work in a specialized area. This was like having the School of Mines under the Bureau of Mines in the United States repeated many times for different industrial ministries. The People's Bank administered a graduate school to train staff for the Bank and its branches in different provinces. The People's University was established to train government officials.

At lower educational levels the government also controlled all schools. Being welfare minded it wanted to raise the level of education for the entire population. By 1978 the literacy rate among population 15 years of age or over was raised to 82%. No private schools were allowed. To see the expansion in education the reader may refer to Table 1 on school enrollment at different educational levels. The enrollment figures have not been adjusted for the increase in population in the corresponding school age.

After 1978 Deng Xiaoping initiated economic reform towards a market-oriented economy. Education was an important part of this reform process. The system of higher education was gradually changed. The main direction was to abandon the Soviet-style higher education system introduced in the 1950s in favor of a more comprehensive and integrated system as practiced in the 1940s. For education at all levels, the government has allowed "citizen-operated" schools to develop and flourish side by side with the schools administered by the governments at all levels.

Table 1.   Student Enrollment by Level of School, 1949 to 1981[a] (10,000 Persons).

| Year | Total | Institutions of higher learning | Secondary Schools[b] | | Primary schools |
			Secondary specialized schools	Regular secondary schools	
1949	2,577.6	11.7	22.9	103.9	2,439.1
1950	3,062.7	13.7	25.7	130.5	2,892.4
1951	4,527.1	15.3	38.3	156.8	4,315.4
1952	5,443.6	19.1	63.6	249.0	5,110.0
1953	5,550.5	21.2	66.8	293.3	5,166.4
1954	5,571.7	25.3	60.8	358.7	5,121.8
1955	5,788.7	28.8	53.7	390.0	5,312.6
1956	6,987.8	40.3	81.2	516.5	6,346.6
1957	7,180.5	44.1	77.8	628.1	6,428.3
1958	9,906.1	66.0	147.0	852.0	8,640.3
1959	10,489.4	81.2	149.5	917.8	9,117.9
1960	10,962.6	96.2	221.6	1,026.0	9,379.1
1961	8,707.7	94.7	120.3	851.8	7,578.6
1962	7,840.4	83.0	53.5	752.8	6,923.9
1963	8,070.1	75.0	45.2	761.6	7,157.5
1964	10,382.5	68.5	53.1	854.1	9,294.5
1965	13,120.1	67.4	54.7	933.8	11,620.9
1966	11,691.9	53.4	47.0	1,249.8	10,341.7
1967	11,539.7	40.9	30.8	1,223.7	10,244.3
1968	11,467.3	25.9	12.8	1,392.3	10,036.3
1969	12,103.0	10.9	3.8	2,021.5	10,066.8
1970	13,181.1	4.8	6.4	2,641.9	10,528.0
1971	14,368.9	8.3	21.8	3,127.6	11,211.2
1972	16,185.3	19.4	34.2	3,582.5	12,549.2
1973	17,096.5	31.4	48.2	3,446.5	13,570.4
1974	18,238.1	43.0	63.4	3,650.3	14,481.4
1975	19,681.0	50.1	70.7	4,466.1	15,094.1
1976	20,967.5	56.5	69.0	5,836.5	15,005.5
1977	21,528.9	62.5	68.9	6,779.9	14,617.6
1978	21,346.8	85.6	88.9	6,548.3	14,624.0
1979	20,789.8	102.0	119.9	5,905.0	14,662.9
1980	20,419.2	114.4	124.3	5,508.1	14,627.0
1981	19,475.3	127.9	106.9	4,859.6	14,332.8

[a] Excludes spare-time schools.
[b] Excludes workers' training schools.
Source: *Statistical Yearbook of China 1981*, p. 451.

The gradual change occurring in education reform, as in economic reform, has taken two and a half decades and is still incomplete, but in both cases we can see what has been accomplished. Higher education has become less specialized, with universities reorganized by including previously separated colleges of medicine, engineering and agriculture and other functional disciplines. While the Ministry of Education in Beijing still controls thirty some major universities, the remaining state universities are under the control of the governments of provinces, cities and townships. The curricula, including economics in particular, have changed to suit the working of a market economy.

Educational institutions at all levels continued to improve not only through the efforts of the central, provincial, and local governments, but also by the efforts from the non-government sectors. "Citizen-operated" or privately financed schools at all levels have become wide spread because there is large demand for them as the Chinese people have become richer and because the schools can be profitable.

In the late 1980s I visited a primary school near Guangzhou that was established privately. The parents had to pay 100,000 RMB, worth about $30,000 at the time, at the beginning of the first year for a six-year primary school education for one child. The investors of this school used the income to build a building on a piece of land leased from the town government at low rent to encourage education. The school was said to be profitable. It was very good in terms of the quality of the teachers and the orderly behavior of the students. Often such schools were established formally by, or in the name of, an association. Associations of all forms sprang up rapidly in China after economic reform started. They are accorded some legal status that a private individual may not possess. They have already invested certain fixed costs in the right to use land or a building, in the establishment of some legal status, in the personal connections of its management and staff, and in the public recognition of the organization. All such investment can be exploited to sponsor a school or another kind of business enterprise.

Non-government schools have grown rapidly not only because they are economically viable, but also because many overseas Chinese are willing to support them. Chinese outside Mainland China have poured money to support all kinds of education in China. Both financial resources and knowledge on administering educational institutions were supplied to China for its benefit, as in the case of foreign investment, except that investment in education is non-profit for most cases. The investor contributes both time and money to improve education in China.

Observers have pointed out that the Chinese education system is deficient partly because the government spends too little on education. They would cite statistics on the amount of government expenditure as a percent of GDP to support this claim. In 1995, public expenditure on education was only 2.5% of GDP in China, as compared with 5.4% in the United States and 5.2% as the world average. These statistics have not taken into account the nonpublic expenditures, contributions by overseas Chinese and other friends, and the spending by the parents to pay tuition in "citizen-operated" schools. Outside contributions to education in certain towns, counties and villages are substantial, including in particular some towns and villages near Hong Kong.

The importance of privately financed education in China and some other countries has been documented in a report *Financing Education — Investments and Returns*, published in 2002 by the United Nations Educational, Scientific and Cultural Organization (UNESCO) and the Organization for Economic Cooperation and Development (OECD), which focuses on sixteen emerging economies. Funds from a wide range of private sources, including individuals and households, contribute much more to education in these countries than in the OECD member states. In Chile, China and Paraguay, for example, more than 40% of the total amount spent on education comes from such private sources. The OECD average is 12%. There has been a rapid development of private education services in these countries, from wholly private, independent institutions to schools that have been subcontracted by governments to non-governmental organizations. In China and Zimbabwe, government-subsidized, community managed schools are said by the above report to be the backbone of the education system. (Author's Note: When I presented the 40% figure for private spending on education in China in the conference, Gary Becker questioned its accuracy. I then supplied some personal observations to support this figure. Even public schools in China at all levels collect tuitions that should be included in private spending, not to mention the large number of nonpublic educational institutions. Data on government and non-government funding of education are found in Tables 20–35 of *China Statistical Yearbook 2003.*)

For the United States, the major concern expressed in *Free to Choose* for primary and secondary education is that the parents have to pay taxes to finance poorly operated public schools and do not have sufficient choice of schools. For college education, there is too much government subsidy while the students should pay their own expenses as a form of investment to prevent waste and misuse of educational resources. In China if privately financed education is wide-spread and accounts for over 40% of total expenditures on education, the concern about public schools using up funds from parents who might prefer to send their children to private schools appears to be less pressing. Furthermore, in the provision of primary and secondary school education the local governments provide choice of schools to the parents. There are usually several public schools of different qualities in the same area. Students can enter a good school if they could pass the required examinations.

For college education, in recent years government policy has been to increase tuition for students and to encourage universities to be more independent financially by seeking ways to generate income, including charging tuition for courses offered to professionals. This policy is consistent with putting the financial burden on students seeking higher education. Thus the education system in China appears to address the concerns expressed in *Free to Choose* in the following two respects. Parents have considerable choice of private and public elementary and secondary schools for their children. Students receiving higher or professional education have to pay for it. At the same time, the government plays an active role in controlling and financing education at all levels.

6.6. Consumer Protection

Chapter 7 of *Free to Choose* on "Who Protects the Consumer" has the following to say: "The market ... must be supplemented by other arrangements in order to protect the consumer from himself and from avaricious sellers, and to protect all of us from the spillover neighborhood effects of market transactions. These criticisms of the invisible hands are valid. The question is whether the arrangements that have been recommended or adopted to meet them are well devised for that purpose, or whether ... the cure may not be worse than the disease." (p. 189) "Every act of [government] intervention establishes positions of power. How that power will be used and for what purposes depend far more on the people who are in the best position to get control of that power and what their purposes are than on the aims and objectives of the initial sponsors of the intervention." (p. 193)

In the process of reforming China's economy, the National People's Congress has passed many new legislations governing economic transactions. Of particular importance for consumer protection are the Product Quality Law of 1993 and the Law on the Protection of the Rights and Interests of Consumers of 1994.[‡]

Product Quality Law of the People's Republic of China stipulates that "producers and sellers are responsible for the product quality according to the provisions of the law." (Article 4) "It is forbidden to forge or infringe upon quality marks...the place of origin ... factory names." (Article 5) The product quality supervision and control departments of the State Council are responsible for the supervision and control of the quality of the products." (Article 8) To insure product quality "enterprises may apply voluntarily for certification of their quality control systems to the product quality supervision and control departments" or "for certification of the quality of their products." (Article 14) "The State shall institute a system of supervision and chiefly random examination to check samples of major industrial products which may be hazardous to

---

[‡] These laws can be found in the website http://www.chinalaw114.com/englishlaw/category.asp?cate=31.

health..." (Article 15) Chapter Three spells out the responsibilities and obligations of producers and sellers to insure the products are safe, have quality and other characteristics as specified, and are certified for quality inspection when necessary. Chapter Four on compensation and damage authorizes the government quality supervision and control departments to order the producers to correct any violation. Chapter Five on penalty provisions states that a violating producer can be ordered to stop production, to pay a fine, to have its license revoked or to take criminal responsibilities if appropriate.

There are now established two administrations in the State Council to carry out the provisions of the Product Quality Law. The General Administration of Quality Supervision, Inspection and Quarantine of the PRC is responsible for certifying the quality control systems of enterprises, issuing certification of product quality, inspecting possibly hazardous products and enforcing all aspects of the Product Quality Law. The State Food and Drug Administration of the PRC is responsible for the approval of food and drug products for sale in the market. We need to collect more evidence to determine whether these two agencies are doing more good in protecting the consumers than harm in slowing innovations. One important function served by certification of product quality is to facilitate the promotion of exports. A few examples of low-quality or mislabeled Chinese products in the world market may hurt the sale of other Chinese products. Some buyers of these products may desire government certification to insure product quality. Even in this case of certification of quality of exports, readers of *Free to Choose* can present arguments in favor of a market solution.

The Law of the People's Republic of China on the Protection of the Rights and Interests of Consumers may have been partly inspired by the United Nations Guidelines for Consumer Protection adopted by the General Assembly on April 9, 1985. Chapter II list the consumer rights, the right to the safety of person in the purchase or use of a commodity, to knowledge of the true facts concerning commodities purchased, to require relevant information of a business operator providing commodities on price, place of origin, specification, to free choice in purchasing commodities or services, to freely choose a business operator providing commodities or services, to compare, appraise and select when freely choosing a commodity or service, to fair dealing, to fair terms of trade, and others. Chapter III specifies obligations of business operators and states, "A business operator providing a commodity or service to a consumer shall perform obligations in accordance with the Product Quality Law of the PRC and other relevant laws and regulations."

It seems that the consumer rights and the business obligations stated above are either unnecessary in the sense that the consumer obviously has such rights unless the government explicitly prohibits them, or redundant in the sense that other laws already cover them.

Chapter VI on dispute resolution provides five ways for consumers to resolve disputes with business operators: (1) negotiate a settlement with the business operator; (2) request a consumer association to mediate; (3) complain to the relevant administrative department; (4) apply to an arbitral body for arbitration; or (5) institute legal proceedings in a People's Court.

For the purpose of this paper a key issue is whether there is a large bureaucracy to enforce the consumer protection laws that may lead to an undue expansion of government power at the expense of economic innovations. To the extent that disputes are settled by other means than through an administrative department, the tendency of expansion of government power is restricted. In China, the population is accustomed to getting help from the government, and cheating by business operators is common. Many consumers welcome intervention by the government to protect their interests from violation by other citizens. If they are free to choose, they may well choose an amount of government protection that is not very different from what is being practiced.

6.7. Macroeconomic Policy

On monetary policy the Chinese government agrees with the Friedman view that the quantity of money is the main instrument to control inflation, and it has applied this policy to maintain fairly stable price levels since the beginning of the PRC. However, there were periods in which the government failed to control the increase in money supply in order to stabilize the price level.

Before the establishment of the PRC, China experienced hyperinflation under the Nationalist Government. The cause of hyperinflation was a large increase in the supply of currency as the government printed money to finance the civil war with the Communists and its other expenditures. Inflation created serious discontent and contributed to the downfall of the Nationalist government. Immediately after the establishment of the PRC, a new currency Renminbi (or the People's currency) was issued in exchange for the existing currency at a reasonable rate.

By control of the supply of Renminbi, the inflation was stopped within, a few months. The general retail price index of China was relatively stable from 1952 to 1978, changing from 82.27 to 100.00. There was only one episode of inflation in early 1960s when the general retail price index increased from 93.08 in 1960 to 112.29 in 1962. We can interpret this increase by the quantity theory of money to which the Chinese government also subscribed as the quantity equation could be found in Marxian economic text books used in Chinese universities. Currency in circulation increased from 9.61 billion in 1961 to 12.57 billion in 1962 while the real GDP index (with 1978 = 100) reduced from 43.9 in 1960 to 30.9 in 1961. The drastic reduction of real GDP was the result of the failure of the Great Leap Forward Movement introduced in 1958.

The control of the quantity of currency in circulation became less strict in the 1980s when the government devoted more attention to the reform of economic institutions and allowed the expansion of credit to finance economic development activities. The first large monetary expansion occurred in 1984 when currency in circulation increased by 50% from January 1984 to January 1985, leading to a 8.8% inflation in 1985. Rapid monetary expansion at annual rates of over 20% continued in the following years until 1988 when the rate of increase was 48%, and the corresponding inflation rate in the fall was about 30% at annual rate. This inflation, together with government corruption, was a cause of discontent and demonstrations in Tiananmen Square that ended in the tragic event of June 4, 1989.

After a slight and short-lived economic slowdown following the Tianenmen incident, the Chinese economy resumed its rapid growth at annual rates of over 10% in 1992 and 1993. The growth was stimulated by the announcement of Deng Xiaoping in Shenzhen in February 1992 to resume and even make bigger steps in reforming the domestic economy and opening China's door to foreign trade and investment. In 1992 money supply increased by 36%. Inflation as measured by the general retail price index reached 13% in 1993 and 22% in 1994.

It was Zhu Rongji as the head of the People's Bank and later as Vice Premier and Premier who tightened the supply of money and credit and stabilized the price level. In fact, China's retail price index was reduced from a high of 121.7 in 1994 to 97.4 in 1998. Monetary policy in the period of the Asian financial crisis of 1997–1999 might even be too restrictive.

On fiscal policy the Chinese government believes in using government expenditures to stimulate the economy during periods of slow growth. A notable example occurred in 1998 during the Asian financial crisis and a period of slower growth in China. Premier Zhu Rongji stated at a press conference on March 19, 1998, that to achieve an 8% growth rate in 1998, the main policy would be to increase domestic demand. He said, "to stimulate domestic demand, we will increase investment in construction of infrastructure, such as railways, highways, agricultural land and water conservancy facilities, municipal facilities, and environmental protection facilities. We will also increase investment in high-tech industries and in the technical renovation of existing enterprises." Thus China adopted the Keynesian way of stimulating aggregate demand by increasing government expenditure, especially in infrastructure-building.

In China increasing government spending served not only to stimulate aggregated demand in periods of slow growth, but also to build infrastructure and other investment projects deemed necessary by the government. Government investment is regarded as important to achieve economic growth, which is not to be left entirely to the decisions of private investors in a market economy.

6.8. The Tide is Turning

I use the same title for this section as the title of the last chapter of *Free to Choose,* because in both cases the subject is trends towards more freedom. In the last chapter of *Free to Choose* the Friedmans suggested ways to increase freedom in the United States. Our discussion in this section is confined to reporting trends towards more freedom in China.

Following the seven topics discussed in this paper, consider first the general trend of economic freedom. We see that the trend is positive as market forces expand. The Chinese people are richer and can enjoy economic freedom to a larger extent. The government has acquired understanding of the working of the market economy and encouraged entrepreneurship. More foreign competition in the domestic market and more opportunities to compete in the world market due to China's WTO membership are pushing the economy forward and will promote more economic freedom.

On political freedom we can see progress towards a more democratic government coming from both the demand for and supply of democratic institutions. On the demand side as the Chinese people have more economic power and become more educated, they will demand to have more freedom and more influence in governmental affairs. On the supply side, the Chinese Communist Party and government officials will become better informed of the modern political systems of the world. As they acquire confidence and ability to govern a modern society in the course of further economic progress, they will be more willing and able to adopt democratic institutions. The change towards a more democratic government has been observed in the spread of popular elections in Chinese villages, the increasingly independent behavior of members of the National People's Congress from directions of the Communist Party and the improvement in the practice of the rule of law partly as a result of China's need to deal with foreign corporations in international trade and investment.

A recent example that the Chinese government can improve from experience is its handling of the problem of SARS (severe acute respiratory syndrome). On June 8, 2003, when the SARS problem had mostly subsided, the *People's Daily* carried an article entitled "SARS, a valuable lesson for the Chinese government to learn." This article states that

"Only by actively upholding the citizens' right, can the government be better supervised by the public and in turn win the trust and respect of those it serves.

"People are made aware of government's views through the information it releases, and they exercise their rightful supervision not only through related government agencies but also through the media, which helps keep the government abreast of public opinion. Therefore, an interactive relationship among government, citizens and the media should be put in place so that the government knows the viewpoints of the people about its policies... The right afforded to the media and law to supervise should be fully guaranteed. When such a right is firmly in place, the activities of those in power come under public scrutiny, thus government and officials become publicly accountable for what they do and therefore more likely to work to higher standards."

The October 2, 2003 issue of *New York Times* (p. A12) carried an article entitled "China's Leader Calls for 'Democratic' Changes" and reported that President and General Secretary Hu Jintao, in an address to the governing Politburo, said the Communist Party must undertake a "sweeping systemic project" to increase public participation in government and enforce the rule of law, and "We must enrich the forms of democracy, make democratic procedures complete, expand citizen's orderly political participation, and ensure that the people can exercise democratic elections, democratic administration and democratic scrutiny."

This appears to be a sign of progress towards a more democratic government. Americans accustomed to a democratic government under a two-party system might find it difficult to appreciate a democratic government under a one-party system, but I believe that election of government officials and of members of the People's

Congress is possible if the Communist Party is willing to put up for electing the best candidates who may be non-Party members for the positions in question. Under a one-party system there are ways that citizens can participate in and influence political affairs. China might well turn out to be an innovator of one form of democratic government under a one-party system.

On the role of government, we observe that the Chinese government is playing its role in maintaining law and order which is essential for the market economy to function. When the government is engaged heavily in economic activities, free choice of the people is provided in China by allowing competition among state enterprises, and among state and private institutions, as in high school education, in health care delivery, in employment, and in the control of pension funds.

On social welfare, a new social security system is being put into effect and gives the people a wider choice that the previous system of entitlement to job security, retirement income and health care, although the performance of the system needs to be further studied. On education we have observed the expansion of privately financed schools and the increase in tuition for students in higher education. Both are expected to continue.

On consumer protection the People's Congress has enacted new laws on product quality and consumer rights along the lines that are set out by a 1984 resolution of the General Assembly of the United Nations. There is as yet no evidence of an unduly large bureaucracy for its administration that hampers innovations in consumer products.

Finally on macroeconomic policies, the Chinese government recognizes the importance of monetary policy and has a fairly good record in controlling the supply of money to maintain a stable price level. At the same time, it practices Keynesian fiscal policy to stimulate the economy and is active in building economic infrastructure and promoting new industries. If we allow for the possibility that the government of a developing country needs to play an active role in maintaining social and economic order, in fostering the development of market institutions and in promoting the development of some new industries, the record in providing freedom to choose in China has been reasonably good and is improving.

Notes

The author acknowledges with thanks helpful comments from Zijun Wang on an early draft of this paper.

References

Chow, Gregory C. (2002). *China's Economic Transformation*. Oxford: Blackwell Publishers.

Chow, Gregory C. (2004). *Knowing China*. Singapore: World Scientific Publishing Company.

Friedman, Milton and Rose. (1979). *Free to Choose: A Personal Statement*. New York: Harcourt Brace Jovanovich.

7

Chinese and American Economic Institutions Reflecting Cultural Differences

Both China and the US practice market economy but their market institutions are different. Institutional differences may help explain the recent economic downturn in the US and the relative economic stability in China. In this essay I attempt to trace the institutional differences to cultural differences in the two countries.

A main feature of a market economy is that it allows profit seeking individuals to benefit the society. Surely both Chinese and Americans are eager to make money. In the US some profit seeking individuals, mainly in finance, have hurt the American economy during the recent financial crisis and economic downturn. In China profit seeking individuals have not caused much instability for the entire economy. Why?

The US economic downturn originates from the housing bubble. Housing bubble is caused by profit seeking. Officials in large financial institutions are eager to make money by taking large risks. They compete with one another in packaging financial derivatives into securities for sale. A financial derivative is a claim that the issuer needs to pay the owner when a specified economic event occurs. Issues of such claims often do not have sufficient capital to pay the owners when prices of assets fluctuate, thus causing financial collapse of their institution. Sellers of home mortgages were active when prices of houses

71

continued to go up. They packaged the mortgages into securities for sale in order to increase profits. When the prices of houses went down and owners of houses could not afford to pay the mortgage loans, the prices of such securities went down and the financial institutions holding such securities collapsed. In the mean time, consumers using credit cards and purchasing houses on credit are also in financial trouble. Such risk taking is a main source of the financial crisis and the ensuring economic downturn in the US.

Chinese financial institutions and consumers are not allowed to take such high risks as in the US. Chinese consumers are required to pay a substantial down payment when purchasing a house, and more substantial for a second house. Even without government requirement they tend to be more conservative in their purchasing behavior as a part of their cultural tradition, as thrift is a part of Confucian ethics. All this explains why a similar financial crisis did not occur in China, although Chinese entrepreneurs have the same desire in seeking profits.

Cultural differences can explain differences in the profit seeking behavior in the two countries. Americans believe in individualism. Chinese believe in collectivism. Americans believe in the Jeffersonian doctrine that the government is the best that governs the least. They distrust the government. By tradition the Chinese respect the government and government officials. The Chinese also respect authority. Although Americans distrust the government, they respect the law and are more law abiding than the Chinese. Confucianism puts less emphasis on law relative to moral judgment which may result in an appeal for authority. In many respects America is ruled by law and China is ruled by people. Many Americans believe that the government is the problem. The Chinese believe that the government is the solution to many problems. In America, businessmen avoid government intervention while they take risks. In China, businessmen make profit by cooperating with the government and the government bureaucrats.

In the course of rapid economic development in recent decades, profit seeking by Chinese entrepreneurs has served as an engine for growth. Chinese bureaucracy is a part of China's market economy as it facilitates the work of the entrepreneurs. Profit seeking in China propels growth because it does not affect the entire system by excessive risk taking. Chinese financial institutions are not allowed to be too big to fail while profit seeking in American financial institutions has created economic instability.

Chinese profit taking can harm many individuals by engaging in illegal activities such as selling false medicine and food products but it does not seriously disturb the functioning of the entire system. Risk taking involving very large sums of money in American is legal but has hurt the functioning of the entire market economy. If so, by new legislation to restrict behavior of businessmen the US government may not have succeeded in preventing future financial problems because there are new ways to get around the new laws. After the current economic downturn US financial institutions have not changed their behavior and have remained on top. The cooperation of Chinese bureaucrats with Chinese entrepreneurs may have contributed to economic growth but it has also involved extensive corruption. Corruption can create serious social instability and the Chinese Communist Party and the Chinese government have tried very hard to stop it.

Different countries can have different forms of market economy. Different forms of market institutions are often the result of differences in culture.

Outflow of Capital and China's Diplomacy

China's integration into the world economy can be discussed from the economic viewpoint or the political viewpoint. This article will emphasize the political and diplomatic aspects. In addition, it will discuss the position of the US for comparison.

A natural consequence of being a large economy is the desire to find opportunities to invest abroad. As Sima Qian in "The Biographies of the Money Markets" of his classic *Record of the Historian* (《史记·货殖列传》第六十九章) keenly observed two thousand years ago, "goods will go where it will fetch more." (故物贱之徵贵) Here goods refer to Chinese capital. Furthermore, as China produces more, there is also a larger demand for natural resources from other countries to use in production.

China's need to import mineral resources from other countries has been subject to criticism. Three years ago, the China Metallurgical Group Corp bid $3.4 billion for the rights to mine deposits near the village of Aynak. The bid was 1 billion more than any of its competitors from Canada, Europe, Russia, the US and Kazakstan. Foreign press reported that over the next 25 years, China allegedly planned to extract about 11 million tons of copper — an amount equal to one third of all the known copper reserves in China.

In December 30, 2009 an article in the New York Times reported on China's activities in Afghanistan, Iraq, Iran and Africa. The extraction of copper in Afghanistan included the building of mining infrastructure (power plant) and railway to ship the copper to China.

There were also extraction of oil in Iraq and purchase of gas from Iran. China was said to be a dominant investor in Pakistan and parts of Africa.

About the Chinese viewpoint I quote from a reply from Premier Wen Jiabao to reporters in Egypt on November 8, 2009, who accused China of trying to control resources and practice the so-called "neu-colonialism" in Africa, "China has always insisted on the principle of not imposing any political conditions in its aid to Africa. Anyone familiar with history knows that China's relation with Africa already began half a century ago. At that time we helped Africa build the Tanzania-Zambia Railway and sent to Africa a large number of medical personnel, without obtaining a drop of oil or any mineral. Today, what has Chinese aid to Africa accomplished? Since 2006, China has aided Africa in eight large projects. The trade volume between China and Africa has increased from 50 billion US dollars to 100 billion. Under the influence of the financial crisis, global foreign investment has declined but Chinese investment in Africa has been increasing this year. Chinese aid has helped Africa establish so many schools, hospitals and clinics, benefiting over 100 million people...."

A book *The Dragon's Gift:The Real Story of China in Africa* (Oxford University Press, 2009) by Deborah Brautigam pointed out the effectiveness of China's foreign aid to Africa. Chinese aids are welcome because China did not impose its values such as democracy and human rights; nor does China intend to use its aid as a bargaining chip for the recipient to join its war against terrorism. In fact developing countries often welcome aid from China more than the aid from the US, because China's has more recent experience in economic development while much of the US experience is outdated.

By comparison the US has interests not only in oil but would like to impose its values on other countries. These include its form of democracy and its advocacy of human rights as well as its war against terrorism. In the recent political upheaval in the Middle East and North Africa, the US changed course from supporting the undemocratic governments of Tunisia, Egypt, Libya, and other Middle Eastern and African countries while China maintained its neutral position of non-interference with internal affairs of other countries. The wars waged by the US in many parts of the world have been criticized even by its own Secretary of Defense, Robert M. Gates as reported in the *New York Times* February 26, 2011: "In my opinion, any future defense secretary who advises the president to again send a big American land army into Asia or into the Middle East or Africa should 'have his head examined,' as General MacArthur so delicately put it."

From the Chinese point of view its relation with developing countries is a part of china's peaceful rise in economic influence. It is sound economics to invest abroad where the rate of return is highest. A large economy always needs mineral resources for production. Foreign aid reflects China's traditional desire to help developing countries. These actions are well justified. The question is whether China is winning or losing friends in the process.

Many countries welcome China's investment and aid, perhaps China can improve its diplomatic relations further by paying even more attention to its image as a friendly and peace loving country. In the case of foreign trade China is criticized by its Asian neighbors for maintaining a low exchange rate of RMB. I suggested in a previous article that China should revaluate the RMB to promote its peaceful rise. In the case of foreign aid we can expect that criticisms from the US and some other developing countries will continue to come, and China will need to explain its actions. Good diplomacy is a necessary part of China's peaceful rise.

CHAPTER 9

Economic Relations Between Brazil and China

China, India and Brazil are the three most rapidly developing countries that people mention when discussing the emerging market economies. China's economic development has been propelled by its exports. Foreign investment has also provided capital and technological knowhow to promote China's economic development. It is interesting to observe how Brazil's export to China and China's investment in Brazil are helping promote Brazil economic development. I had an opportunity to observe the economic relations between Brazil and China in a recent conference on "China and the World Economy" in Rio de Janeiro on March 17 and 18, 2011.

The two sponsors of the conference are Getulio Vargas Foundation (FGV) and Vale. The former is the leading Brazilian higher education institution founded in 1944 that offers regular courses of economics, business administration, law, social sciences and information technology management. It is considered by Foreign Policy magazine to be a top-5 "policymaker think-tank" worldwide. Vale is the second-largest mining company in the world. It is also the largest producer of iron ore and the second largest of nickel. The conference was attended by scholars, businessmen and government officials as well as students. The purposes of the conference were to learn more about the Chinese economy and determine the role that Brazil can play in its economic relation with China.

The two-day conference has 6 speakers per day, plus the Dean of the School of Economics of FGV and the Director of Investor Relations of Vale as two luncheon speakers. Among the 12 speakers 10 are invited from outside: Gregory Chow (邹至庄) of Princeton University on "China as a leader of the world economy;" Eswar Prasad of Cornell University on "Sustaining the Chinese growth miracle: a delicate balancing act;" Yasheng Huang (黄亚生) of MIT on "Dynamics and challenges in the Chinese economy;" Barry Naughton of the University of California, San Diego on "Chinese economic policy since the global financial crisis: the new state activism;" Jonathan Anderson of UBS Investment Research on "The Sector that wouldn't die;" Raghuram G. Rajan of the University of Chicago on "The global trade imbalances and what role China might play;" Liqun Jin (金立群) of China Investment Corporation on "The future of the Chinese economy;" Nicholas Lardy of the Peterson Institute for International Economics on "Is China's growth sustainable?"; Luis Serven of the World Bank on "China: international finance and exchange rates;" Jianping Mei (梅建平), Cheung Kong Graduate School of Business on "China's financial growth from asset price perspective." The topics presented are interesting. From this conference I have learned certain aspects of the relationship between Brazil and China, and certain views of the Brazilian government and Brazilian people concerning such a relationship. Perhaps such attitudes apply to other developing countries that are under the sphere of influence of the US.

Exports to China have helped promote Brazil's economic growth. Vale has signed a contract to deliver iron ore to China for 19 years. This shows how far-sighted economic planning in China is. China's Investment Corporation has invested in Vale to insure that the future supply of iron ore will be forthcoming. Vale benefits from the inflow of capital from China. In the mean time the Brazilians are careful about the possible objections from the US. China has tried to obtain assets from the US that are vital to its economic interest but the US has refused to sell some of the assets that are of security interest. Similarly US may object to China's attempt to purchase assets of strategic importance from countries that are under the US influence.

The President of FGV, Carlos Ivan Simonsen Leal, who received a PhD degree in economics from Princeton in the early 1980s and was my former student, asked the first question after my presentation. He asked my assessment of the chance of a military conflict between China and the US when the two countries will be competing with each other as economic leaders in the world. I was somewhat surprised by this question. As citizens of smaller countries living close to the US, South Americans feel that they are under the sphere of American influence. Sensing the aggression of the US, they envision the possibility of American aggression towards China if the US interest is threatened by the rise of China. Having lived in the US since 1948 and being an American citizen I consider the US to be a friendly country towards China and to be interested in cooperating with China in spite of possible conflicts in their economic and military interests . War between the two countries is extremely unlikely from my viewpoint. This viewpoint may not be shared by some readers of this article and is certainly not shared by Brazilians.

I begin to appreciate the viewpoint of the South Americans who are under the influence of the US. They have experienced American aggressions but could not defend themselves. They are careful in every move in economic relation with China for fear of criticisms or even adverse actions by the US. They consider US as a strong power that likes to impose its policy on South American countries.

To summarize the Brazilians are eager to strengthen its relation with China, but are careful not to offend the US. Trade between Brazil and China is advantageous to both. China's investment in Brazil including a stake in Vale is mutually beneficial. But the economic relation is delicate from the Brazilian point of view. Brazil also uses China to balance its dependence on the US, but there is fear in having a close economic relation with China. In a previous article "Outflow of Capital and China's Diplomacy" (《中资外流与中国外交》) I discussed the economic and investment relation from the Chinese point of view. This article supplements that discussion by presenting the viewpoint of a trading partner of China's. This discussion may apply to China's economic relations with other developing countries as well. I believe that the Chinese government is well aware of the sensitivities of the developing countries and of the competitiveness of the Americans in its relations with other countries.

CHAPTER 10

India's Model of Rapid Economic Development

India's model of rapid economic development is illustrated in a recent article in the *New York Times* dated June 9, 2011 (p. A1). The article reported on the rapid development of the city Gurgaon, located about 15 miles south of the national capital New Delhi. The city barely existed two decades ago, but now it has a population of 1.5 million. There are 26 shopping malls, seven golf courses, numerous luxury shops, and automobile showrooms selling Mercedes-Benzes and BMWs. Apartment towers are sprouting like concrete weeds, and a futuristic commercial hub called Cyber City houses many of the world's most respected corporations. Other similar cities have been developed as well. Such developments have occurred despite a malfunctioning government in the area, because the functions ordinarily provided by the government have been provided by the private sector as described below.

In this article I will show how this Indian model of economic growth fits into the theory of rapid economic growth that I have discussed often in previous writings. In my theory there are three factors contributing to rapid economic growth, namely, an abundance of high-quality human capital, a functioning market economy and the existence of a technology gap that enables the developing country to catch up. These three factors are sufficient to explain the rapid economic growth in China in the last three decades, in Japan before and after WWII, and in the four dragons of Hong Kong, Singapore,

Taiwan and South Korea in the 1960s to early 1980s. In this theory I did not specify the nature of the government, for example, whether it has a Western democracy or not. The examples of rapid development cited above do not have a Western democracy. Nor did I specify the effectiveness of the government. I do mention a functioning market economy, implying that the government cannot be so bad as to impair the effective functioning of the market economy.

The India model helps clarify my theory in three important respects:

1. Human capital is very important as the India story illustrates. The rapid development described above is due to the very able Indian entrepreneurs and blue color workers who have built the cities including Gurgaon. Such human capital has been developed in India through many years of its history.

2. The functioning of the market, including the degree of participation of the government, can be flexible. China has a strong and effective government. The Chinese government often allows the market to decide which functions are public by allowing private enterprises to compete with existing public enterprises in many sectors of the economy. In the case of India the government is not effective in providing the services which are often provided by the government in other countries. In the development of Gurgaon and other cities, the private sector has taken over such functions as the building of infrastructure, the provision of electricity and water, of "public" transportation, of "public" security, of "public" elementary schools and of garbage pickup. Almost any goods and services that are provided publicly in other countries have been provided privately in the rapid development of new cities in India.

3. Corruption may exist side by side with rapid economic development. It has existed when China experienced rapid economic development in the last three decades. However it cannot be too serious as to affect political stability and interfere with the effective functioning of a market economy. Corruption also exists in the Indian government, but in areas when the government does not have effective control, such as the city of Gurgaon, government corruption is irrelevant.

CHAPTER 11

Will the Russian Economy Grow Rapidly?

In previous chapters I have discussed three of the four emerging market economies known as BRICs: Brazil, India and China of course. This article will briefly discuss the growth of the Russian economy. I will present some statistics about the growth rates of GDP since economic reform started in 1990 and explain what is behind the growth rates. Then I will answer the question at what rate the Russian economy can be expected to grow in the next 15 years or so.

After economic reform started in 1990 to change the planned economy to a market economy, Russia experienced large decreases in real GDP for eight years. Under the presidency of Vladimir Putin from 1999 to 2008, real GDP grew at 6.5%, 10%, 5.7%, 4.9%, 7.3%, 7.2%, 6.4%, 8.2%, 8.5% and 5.2% respectively, averaging 7% per year and making Russia the 6th largest economy in the world in terms of purchasing power parity. On a per capita basis, Russian GDP was US$14,919 in 2009, making Russia the 38th richest in the world.

In 2007, Russia's real GDP finally exceeded that of 1990 as the economy had recovered from its decline resulting from mistaken policies for economic reform. To judge the 7% growth rate during the years 1999–2008 as compared with the approximately 10% growth rate for China, one has to keep in mind the effect of recovery. It is fair to say that the rate of economic growth in Russia in recent years is fairly high but below the rates in China and India.

To understand this fact, I appeal to the three important economic factors contributing to rapid economic growth in developing countries, namely, the abundance of high-quality human capital, a set of functioning market institutions, and the early stage of economic development that enables the economy to catch up at a high speed. I have used these three factors to explain the rapid economic growth in Japan before and after WWII, in the four dragons of East Asia (Hong Kong, Singapore, Taiwan and South Korea) from the 1960s to the 1980s, in China since the 1980s and in India since the 1990s. If the rate of growth in Russia is somewhat below that of China and India, we can attribute the difference to these three factors.

On the first factor, human capital in Russia as evolved from its historical tradition is as good as in China and India. On the second factor, the market institutions in Russia are perhaps not as good as those in China and India. It is more difficult for Russian entrepreneurs to strive than for Chinese and Indian entrepreneurs. The government has not established policies as favorable to the entrepreneurs and government officials do not cooperate with entrepreneurs in establishing new businesses as in China. The legal system is less favorable to private business. Taxation and business regulations are unpredictable, and legal enforcement of private business agreements is weak. Attitudes left over from the Soviet period will take many years to overcome. Government decisions affecting business have often been arbitrary and inconsistent. Crime has increased costs for both local and foreign businesses. Although the Russian government is in control of rich oil resources, and such resources account for a substantial part of total output, this can affect total output but not its rate of increase.

Russia has serious problems of corruption as in China and India. The corruption level was high in the 90s and steadily grew during the 2000s as in China. It is not a problem of laws, because Russian laws concerning business are in fact quite good by international standards as in China. Also similar to China, the problem is law enforcement.

To project economic growth in the next ten to fifteen years, one needs to consider the three factors in operation. The third factor will lead gradually to a slower rate as an economy develops and its distance from the most advanced economy narrows, but this is a slow process.

Human capital as the first factor depends on a country's historical and cultural tradition. It can be changed only very slowly by improving the education system. First, efforts to improve the educational system takes effect slowly as the education of a single individual takes time and only a fraction of the total labor force is affected. Furthermore, the number of years of schooling for an individual is only one aspect of human capital which depends on family education and historical tradition. Thus the effect of possible change in human capital on economic growth in the next decade or so is small.

Finally, market economic institutions as the second factor can be changed. If the government and the legal institutions in Russia can be improved to make the market institutions more favorable to entrepreneurship and more suitable for economic development, the rate of economic growth can be increased to some extent.

CHAPTER 12

Comparing Economic Developments in Taiwan and Mainland China

On August 1, 2011 I gave a lecture in Taipei on China's economic development, including a comparison between the economic developments of Taiwan and mainland China. Some of the observations are given below.

Both economies have been successful in developing a set of functioning market institutions.

12.1. Similarities

1. Through economic liberalization in Taiwan and economic reform in the mainland, both have allowed market incentives to operate and encouraged development of private enterprises. Banking liberalization was slow in both, but today banking has been liberalized. Private banking flourished in the 1920s and 1930s in China, but both went backwards in limiting the functioning of private banking, and then later liberalized the operation of banking and financial institutions again.

2. The role of the government is more important than in many Western economies. This is the result of history in both economies. In mainland an additional factor was the practice of central planning up to the early 1980s. In Taiwan the ideas of economic planning were prevailing until KY Yin changed the mind of Chiang Kai-shek in the late 1950s. From the historical perspective, note the parallel between Minister Liang Yansun in late Qing Dynasty in guiding the development of Bank of

Communications in 1907 and Minister KT Li in encouraging the establishment of the very successful Taiwan Semiconductor Manufacturing Company in 1987.

Economic planning is still practiced in both, such as the National Development and Reform Commission in mainland preparing the 5-year plans, and Taiwan's Council for Economic Planning and Development preparing 6-year plans.

12.2. Differences

1. The government of mainland China has become a more important player in the market economy as a result of the tradition of central planning. When market reform started, the people in China were poor and the commercial banking system was not well-established to provide capital to the private sector to establish new enterprises, so as to fill the need of the market economy. Township and village governments established their "public" enterprises, which are financially independent, to fill the need of the market. State-owned enterprises were also financially independent during enterprise reform of the late 1990s. The Shanghai government has built up stores, restaurants and hotels in the former French Concession and other areas.

Government enterprises in mainland are more profit oriented, including the former TVEs and the current enterprises of the Shanghai government. As long as government enterprises are financially independent, they serve the market economy as well as private enterprises. Why should entrepreneurship be restricted to private enterprises? Because mainland governments at national, provincial and local levels were much larger to begin with, government officials tired to find ways to take advantages of market reform. They use their power to participate in the activities of a market economy.

2. The political systems in the two economies are different. Democracy in Taiwan is less efficient in formulating economic policies as there is much disagreement among members of the Legislative. A more authoritative government in the 1950s to the early 1980s was much effective in formulating and executing economic policies.

3. Market institutions in both economies can be improved.

a. Universities in both can be improved by having more autonomy in decision making. In the mainland the power of the Ministry of Education carried over from the period of central planning still remains to a considerable extent. This prevents university presidents and leading administrators from exercising their autonomy and initiative to develop the university with its own characteristics. In Taiwan, the salary scale of faculty members is not flexible as in the mainland. Without paying internationally competitive salaries, universities and government research institutions in Taiwan cannot recruit first-rate scholars from the world market or even retain some of their own first-rate faculty and research personnel.

b. Free entry of private enterprises is very good in both economies, but is perhaps better in the mainland. The mainland government has encouraged and supported very talented people to establish successful business enterprises. An outstanding example is the support given to Dr. Shi Zhengrong in the establishment of Suntech.

c. Restrictions of business activities may be more extensive in Taiwan than in the mainland. A main reason is political considerations. In the past, investment by Taiwan entrepreneurs in setting up certain businesses in China was restricted. This included attempts by the late leading entrepreneur Wang Yongching in setting up factories to produce plastic products in the mainland. The situation has improved. However, the differences in political opinions among the residents in Taiwan are interfering with the development of the Taiwan economy. Economic uncertainty is always bad for business investments. As it has been generally observed, the change of policies between the government under President Chen Suibian and President Ma Yingjeou has affected economic activities in Taiwan. The uncertainty surrounding the coming presidential election is also affecting business activities. In the mainland the succession of a new set of political leaders is unlikely to affect the economic activities in China, including trade and investment between these two economies.

In the 1980s, mainland had more to learn from Taiwan in promoting market institutions. Today Taiwan perhaps has more to learn from the mainland on how to foster market economic activities. There is more dynamism in certain parts of the mainland economy. People in Taiwan need to free themselves from political considerations and concentrate on developing their economy.

PART 2

Economic Issues

CHAPTER 13

Problems Facing the Chinese Economic System

In this chapter I will discuss briefly five problems facing the Chinese economic system: corruption, income disparity, education, healthcare, and environmental degradation.

13.1. Corruption

Corruption in China is widespread and has gotten worse in the last decade. By corruption I mean government officials taking advantage of their economic power to obtain illegitimate personal gains from the public and private institutions or government organizations. The economic power is derived from the economic assets under their control such as financial assets of state-owned banks or land. Power is also denied from their authority in granting economic assets such as licenses or permits.

Corruption has increased in the course of China's economic development, because both the demand for and supply of it have increased. Demand has increased because more people need government approvals to establish and operate their expanding businesses, and more products and international trading need licenses and permits. Supply has increased because the bureaucracy has expanded to deal with a growing economy and the bureaucrats have more tasks to perform in operating government enterprises and in approving new products and granting licenses.

The Communist Party leadership and the central government of China have tried very hard to control corruption. We often read in the newspapers that a certain corrupt official received a death sentence. Such effort has not reduced corruption because the fundamental economic reason for its existence still remains. From an economic point of view, one can imagine trying to reduce corruption by treating its root, namely reducing the economic power of government officials. First, one could streamline the procedures for the establishment and operation of businesses by reducing the number of approvals and inspections required. This is not easy to achieve because of the vested interests of the officials who benefit from such power. Secondly, one can also think of reducing the steps for the approval of new drugs. In traditional China, producing herbal medicine required no license and was not protected by patents. People were free to reproduce if they could discover the way. Some economists question the usefulness of the modern Western system of patents as justified by the necessity to encourage research. Patents have two serious disadvantages. Consumers lose the benefits of getting new medicine early and at a lower cost. Other potential inventors are hindered in their research for fear of infringing on existing patents. In the Chinese case, officials receive bribes in millions of RMB for the approval of drugs to be sold in the market. Third, a most important source of corruption is in the approval of land for urban development. Since land is publicly owned under the Chinese Constitution, it is in fact controlled by government bureaucrats. In their term of office these bureaucrats would try to approve the land under their control for development to receive benefit, rather than keeping most of it undeveloped to wait for future opportunities as in the case of private ownership. However, to change the public ownership of land is almost impossible politically.

In sum, we can say that corruption is rooted in the economic power of the bureaucrats. Hence to reduce their corruption we need to reduce the economic power. In the three important sources of economic power that we have discussed the political feasibility of reducing the power is nil. Thus corruption is expected to last for some time to come. Corruption has created social discontent but is not serious enough to generate major social instability, because most Chinese have learned to live with it while getting rich under the current system.

13.2. Income Disparity and Rural Poverty

In China the income disparity between the urban rich and the rural poor has been widened in the last fifteen years. The per capita income of the urban population has been growing at an annual rate of 7.5%, while that of the rural population has been growing at 5.5%. This creates a widening income gap between the two groups. Note, however, that the livelihood of rural population has also been advancing at a rapid rate, although not as rapid as the urban population.

There are three major components of the rural poverty problem. First, as pointed out, the rural population has experienced a widening income gap in comparison with the urban rich. This is not a serious problem because the rural population has also been getting rich. The percentage of rural population below the poverty line defined as per capita income below 600 yuan in 2003 prices was reduced from 12% in 1985 to 9% in 1990 and further to 3.5% in 2003.

The second component is the unfavorable treatment of the rural residents by the central government as compared with the urban residents. The government has spent less on infrastructure investment in rural areas. It invested only a limited amount to improve agricultural productivity. It provided less welfare benefits including education and healthcare subsidies to rural residents. The migrant workers from rural to urban areas do not receive the same educational and medical care benefits as the urban residents. The procurement prices for farm products paid by the government were often below market prices, while the farmers were not allowed to sell their products in the market. Note, however, that under the "Three-farm program" for the improvement of farming, farmers and rural areas initiated in 2001 the government has started to increase its spending to improve rural education, healthcare and infrastructure building. It also abolished all taxes on farmers in 2005.

The third and most serious component of the rural poverty problem is the mistreatment of the rural population by village Communist Party secretaries who have power to control the population in his village. There have been illegal levies for road construction and for the building or maintenance of local schools while there was no need. More importantly there has been the frequent takeover of land that was legally assigned to farmers without adequate compensation. Thousands of demonstrations have taken place in recent years without being reported in newspapers. Although the right to keep the land assigned to farmers under contract is protected by law, this law is often violated in practice. Much discontent among the rural population has been generated but the central government is not able to control the behavior of local party officials who are protected by officials above them. I once suggested that the media be given more freedom to expose the offenders, but my suggestion may not be easily accepted because the degree of freedom given to the press is an important matter in China, and the Communist Party gives it many serious considerations in the exercise of leadership.

13.3. Education

Two aspects of the problem of income disparity are the inadequate education and healthcare that the poor residents in rural area receive. Although China has an official policy of providing compulsory education of nine years, in reality many children of school age do not receive nine years of education because the central government does not financially support this policy and leaves the financial responsibility to the local governments. Government of poor villages do not have enough financial resources to provide free compulsory education. As a result many poor families spend a large fraction of their income to pay for tuition and fees for their children attending local schools. In China there are many private schools at all levels because the government allows and even encourages these "people-operated" schools to flourish to supplement the public schools, but poor families cannot afford sending their children to these schools. Over 40% of total education expenditures in China are financed by non-government sources including the payment of tuition. This illustrates the problem of inadequate financing of education for children of poor families.

The inequality of education opportunities among the rich and the poor is a most serious part of the income disparity problem as discussed above. It affects income inequality for future generations and also hinders the selection of the most able young people in China for personal development. Due to the improvement in tax collection, the national government has received revenues that have grown at an even higher rate than GDP because of improvement in the tax collection system. Total education expenditure by the central government has kept up with the increase in revenue but much of it is spent for higher education, while leaving the responsibility of financing primary school education to local governments and individuals. Although in the last few years the central government has increased its subsidy to local governments for education, inequality of education opportunities still persists and the children of very poor families do not get educated. In many rural families the oldest child, especially a girl, is not supported by her family to go to school beyond the primary school and is asked to work to support her younger siblings so that they will have a better education.

13.4. Healthcare

Like education, health care is the responsibility of the government but the central government does not finance most of it and leaves its financing to local governments; the central government has devoted more resources to the urban population in healthcare than the rural population.

In rural China before economic reform health care provision was good given its low level of income. Under the commune system healthcare was provided under a three-tier system with barefoot doctors (country doctors without much formal medical education) taking care of minor illnesses which occurred most often, local clinics taking care of patients that the barefoot doctors could not treat, and hospitals taking care of more serious illnesses. This was an economically efficient way of utilizing medical resources. As a result the death rate in China was reduced from 17 per thousand in 1952 to 6.34 in 1980, and life expectancy was increased from 40.8 years in the early 1950s, to 49.5 in the early 1960s and 65.3 in the late 1970s. After economic reform, with the introduction of private farming and the disintegration of the communes, financing and provision of healthcare have been left to market forces. Healthcare is paid for privately. The rural population in some poor areas cannot afford to pay for medical care, and often do not go to get treatment when they get sick. The government is trying to establish a Collective Medical System (CMS) as a form of collective insurance for each rural resident to pay for medical expenses. A policy announced in 2005 was to have each individual insured for 50 yuan per year, with the central government paying 20 yuan, the local government paying 20 yuan and the rural family itself paying the remaining 10 yuan. As of the middle of 2006 only about 30% of the rural families joined the CMS. A reason is that many rural residents do not trust the government in having paid 40 yuan for the stated purpose because of their experiences in past dealings with local government officials. In 2006 the government introduced a policy of achieving 80% participation of CMS program but the degree of actual participation as of mid-2007 was still below this goal.

Healthcare for the urban population has been better since economic reform. Previously the employing units provided healthcare for their employees. Because the reform of industrial enterprises was a slow process, unlike the collapse of the commune system, most employees remained protected for many years. In the mean time the government introduced an insurance system with the employer and the employee each paying 6% of the salary. In addition the hospitals of the employing units such as state enterprises and universities remain in operation, unlike the barefoot doctors who went into private practice and the local clinics which were no longer financed under the commune system.

Healthcare is considered a major problem in China because price has been rising at the rate of about 12% per year in the last ten years and quality of service has deteriorated with long waiting lines in good hospitals. The reason for the rapid rise in the price of medical care is that the quantity supplied per person has remained constant since

1995, but the demand for healthcare has increased rapidly because of the increase in per capita real income. The reason for supply per capita to have been constant is the policy of public supply of healthcare under which the local governments are given the responsibility to provide healthcare. We can measure the quantity supplied by the total national expenditure on healthcare divided by a price index of healthcare, and further divided by population to convert it to a per capita quantity, with all statistics given in *China Statistical Yearbook*. We can also measure it by the number of hospital beds per 10,000 population or the number of doctors per 10,000 population. Using all of these statistics the quantity supplied had been constant since 1995, while the quantities of all other consumer goods and services have increased, because the local governments do not have sufficient funds to provide healthcare in line with the growth of the local economy. They would rather use the funds for economic development. A simple solution to the shortage of supply is to allow or even encourage the entry of private hospitals which should be subject to the same regulations on standards that govern the existing public hospitals. Unlike the case of education where private schools are allowed or even encouraged, the Chinese government still maintains the notion that healthcare should be publicly supplied. The entry of private hospitals would increase supply while providing competition to public hospitals to lower the prices and improve the quality of their services.

In mid 2007 there were signs that the central government may change its policy to allow for competition. There was a debate in China among expert consultants appointed by the Chinese government to examine whether the government should spend its healthcare expenditures by giving it to the public hospitals or to the individuals in the form of additional insurance coverage, so that they can choose the hospital for treatment, whether public or private. The debate was framed in terms of whether to finance the demand side or the supply side of healthcare. An executive order from the State Council was issued in mid July 2007 to establish several experimental stations for financing the demand side and even allowing for some private hospitals. This was an encouraging development for someone like the author who has championed for the establishment of private hospitals in the last two years through communications with top government leaders. The arguments for supporting the demand side are the same as those favoring the use of school vouchers to allow the parents to choose the school rather than financing public schools directly to supply public education.

13.5. Energy and Environment

The problem of environmental degradation is common to all developing countries which try to increase its output and consumption because production and consumption require the use of energy, and the use of energy affects the environment. The effects are air pollution, water pollution and emission of CO_2 that cause global warming. Furthermore the use of energy from exhaustible resources can create energy shortage in the future.

The air and water in China, especially in the urban areas, are among the most polluted in the world. According to a report of the World Health Organization (WHO) in 1998, of the ten most polluted cities in the world, seven can be found in China. China's water is polluted by the disposal of waste. Water beds of several important cities including Beijing and Shanghai are low, causing shortage of supply of well water. Supply of waters from rivers including the Yellow River and the Yangtze River are running short because of diversion to agriculture production and electricity generation along the sources. In terms of energy use, China's energy intensity as measured by thousand Btu per 1990 dollars of output was high, being 36 thousand, as compared with 21 thousand for Indonesia, 13 thousand for South Korea, 4 thousand for Japan and 11 thousand for the United States, because of differences in output of these countries and in energy intensities in producing the same products.

CO_2 emissions result in climate changes which are affecting the world's physical and biological systems. As of 2001 China accounted for 13 percent, Western European 16 percent and the US 24 percent of the world's energy related carbon emission. By 2007 China has taken over the US for the first time for the first time as the world's top producer of greenhouse gases. China's environmental policies aim at cutting energy costs and reducing local pollution, rather than reducing carbon emissions, the effects of which are not felt at present.

The Chinese central government has been aware of the environmental problems and has made serious attempts to protect and improve China's environment. The 1982 Constitution included important environmental protection provisions. Article 26 of the Constitution requires that "the state protects and improves the environment in which people live and the ecological environment. It prevents and controls pollution and other public hazards." This article formed the basis of the Water Pollution Prevention and Control Law of 1984, the Air Pollution Prevention and Control Law of 1987, the Water and Soil Conservation Law of 1991, the Solid Waste Law of 1995, the Energy Conservation Law of 1997 and several important international agreements including the Kyoto and Montreal Protocol.

China's environmental protection policies include (1) restricting the quantities of outputs, especially those that are environmentally polluting and high-energy consuming, by tightening land use and credit supply, (2) setting environmental standards for production, especially in new projects, (3) improving method of production to make it environmentally friendly, including the promotion of the use of hydropower, wind and atomic energy, (4) imposing heavy penalties to emissions of sulfur dioxide and encouraging the building of equipment to capture sulfur dioxide (5) imposing a tax on high-sulfur coals to reduce the use of coal and to encourage a switch to cleaner burning fuels, (6) experimenting in some cities with a system of emissions trading for sulfur dioxide, similar to that used in the United States and (7) introducing technologies that will treat wastewater, prevent air pollution and improve environmental monitoring systems.

The most serious problem for China's well-intended environmental policies is the failure in implementation. As an illustration, on Friday, May 8, 2007, Premier Wen Jiabao made a speech stating that the current macro-control policy must focus on energy conservation and emission reduction in order to develop the economy while protecting the environment. The Chinese government has set a target of reducing energy consumption for every 10,000 yuan of GDP by 20% by 2010 [or 4% per year], while pollutant discharge should drop by 10%. However this policy was not successfully implemented, with the actual rate of reduction being 1.6% instead of the targeted 4% in 2006.

The implementation of environmental policies especially in pollution control fails mainly because local government officials often do not cooperate in law enforcement as they are interested in increasing output of their own regions. The central government needs to establish and monitor a set of clear cut environmental standards and severely punish the provincial governor for serious violations in his province to the extent of removing him from office. If so the provincial governor would apply the same policy to enforce environmental standards in cities and counties in his province by similarly punishing the officials below him. However the Communist Party leadership may not have such a strong resolve and thus China's environmental laws will not be effectively enforced for some time to come. In the mean time the central government can try to protect the environment by reducing energy intensity in production and increasing the use of clean energy through the provision of economic incentives for energy saving and the reduction of the relative price of clean energy. How to design a set of incentives to achieve this in practice remains a very challenging problem for the government. The end result is that the quality of China's environment will continue to deteriorate in the near future until the country is rich enough and the government is determined enough to spend more resources for environmental protection.

A second important problem is to achieve a multinational agreement to limit the emission of CO_2. If the level of carbon dioxide reaches twice the level existing before the Industrial Revolution, great climate instability will occur. How to achieve an international consensus to reduce the rate of increase with each country taking its fair share so as not to exceed the above critical level is a most pressing problem today, but a politically feasible solution is difficult to achieve.

13.6. Conclusion

Among the problems affecting the functioning of the Chinese economic system, I have discussed corruption, income disparity and rural poverty, education, healthcare and the environmental protection. All these problems are characteristics of a rapidly developing economy where the government has not been able to control the undesirable consequences of economic growth. Corruption, and to a lesser extent exploitation of peasants by local Party officials and violation of environmental protection laws are political problems that are difficult to resolve. Education and healthcare problems require simple changes in economic policies that can be easily achieved if the central government is willing. Fortunately for China, these problems will not do sufficient harm to create serious social instability that would impede further growth. In other words, the rising China will keep on rising.

References

Chow, Gregory C. (2006, June). "Demand for Education in China." *International Economic Journal*, 20:2, pp. 129–147.

Chow, Gregory C. (2006, August). "An Economic Analysis of Healthcare in China." Princeton University: Center for Economic Policy Studies Working Paper No. 132.

Chow, Gregory C. (2006, September). "Rural poverty in China: Problem and policy." Princeton University: Center for Economic Policy Studies Working Paper No. 134.

Chow, Gregory C. (2007, July). "Corruption from an economic point of view," (in Chinese). *Hong Kong Economic Journal Monthly*, No. 364, pp. 62–63.

Chow, Gregory C. (2007, July). "China's Energy and Environmental Problems and Policies." Princeton University: Department of Economics, mimeo.

CHAPTER 14

Directions for Economics Education and Research in China*

The Chinese Economists Society held its annual meeting in Xiamen in June 2010. An important topic to be discussed is directions for economics education and research in China, the topic of this chapter. I would like to discuss two aspects of this topic, importing economics knowledge from abroad and exploring the frontier of economic knowledge in China.

14.1. Importing Economics Knowledge from Abroad

What are we importing from the US? What is in the forefront of economics in the US? In recent years economics in the US has become more theoretical and less relevant to important real life economic problems of the world. Its development is similar to the development of pure mathematics. Adam Smith pointed out the efficiency of the market economy as if it were guided by an invisible hand. Modern economists have proved the existence and optimality of competitive equilibrium in a market economy. Much of the subject has become purely intellectual exercises but it is a highly respected subject as in the case of pure mathematics. Whether some parts of pure mathematics are relevant to solving actual problems is not a question of interest to mathematicians just as whether some

---

* Addressed to the annual meeting of the Chinese Economists Society in Xiamen in June, 2010.

parts of theoretical economics are relevant to solving real life problems is not a concern for many economists. Of course, some parts of pure mathematics or of theoretical economics may turn out to be useful unexpectedly.

On the relevance of current research in the forefront of economics, there are interesting ideas being pursued in different directions, and many are not in the realm of pure theoretical economics but deals with economic behavior in microeconomics, macroeconomics, financial economics, international economics, and in areas overlapping with sociology, psychology and political science. However, as judged by its usefulness in solving economic problems facing developing countries, these ideas are of secondary importance to the well-known and basic ideas such as supply and demand. Recently discovered knowledge is only a small part of the total stock of useful knowledge in economics and other fields of science. Important problems are solved much more often by knowledge already explained in undergraduate or first-year graduate textbooks. It is in this sense that knowledge acquired in the forefront of economic research is less relevant than existing knowledge in the solution of urgent real life economic problems.

Given the nature of the product that we are importing, how and how well are we importing it from the US? We have established new schools or research institutes and improved existing schools of economics and finance. Much funding has been provided. American professors are appointed dean of the schools or director of the institutes. American PhDs have been recruited to serve on the faculty. The administration of some of the best schools has been modernized. Faculty performance is judged by their publications in international journals. Some of these efforts are extremely successful. We can expect that in the near future some of these schools or institutes will become world-class.

14.2. Exploring the Frontier of Economic Knowledge in China

We should first recognize our comparative advantage in the production of economic knowledge. Economists in China live in the most rapidly growing economy which is assuming a leadership position in the world economy but at the same time is facing poverty and other problems in many parts of the country. The environment provides interesting topics of research. Great advancement in economics has come from important historical developments. Keynes' *General Theory* was stimulated by the Great Depression. Milton Friedman's school of market economics rode the wave of economic prosperity after World War II. Needless to say, ideas of great minds affect world history also. Chinese and world history is on the side of Chinese economists. We should take full advantage of this golden opportunity to pursue research and teaching in China.

The topics of research should naturally be topics about the Chinese economy, rather than topics derived from the forefront of economic research in the US. We should try to understand economic behavior and economic institutions in China where the economy is changing rapidly. The teaching and research in economics should be problem motivated rather than tools motivated. A Chinese economist living in this stimulating environment should observe the environment carefully and allow it to present important topics for research.

Interesting topics are not difficult to find. In the last two to three years in the process of writing newspaper articles I found a number of interesting topics. The articles are now published in a book, *Interpreting China's Economy* «中国经济随笔» by CITIC Press. Other economists in China pursuing similar and other topics in the future will provide deeper analysis with more originality.

Policy problems constitute a major area of research. There are so many economic problems today awaiting solutions. Some are recognized by the Chinese government. It has urged economists in China to study problems facing the Chinese economy rather than or besides doing research for publication in international journals. To name a few, there are problems of western development, rural poverty, healthcare, education, inflation, population, development of alternative energy and environmental protection. More problems will appear as the economy evolves.

I am not suggesting that all economists in China should work on problems facing the Chinese economy. Since there are both theoretical and applied areas for Chinese economist to the effort to assume leadership in economics education and research there is plenty of room for individual economists to pursue their interest in one part or the other.

On teaching, the material for teaching should naturally be integrated with the topics of research. The topics of research will be generated by observing and experiencing the economic problems of China. Basic economics should be taught within a Chinese institutional setting rather than by using textbooks translated from popular US textbooks. Chinese economists should write their own textbooks, with basic theoretical material borrowed from US textbooks when appropriate. Research results on the Chinese economy should be integrated into the textbooks for undergraduate and graduate students to provide real-life examples to make the subject interesting to the students. On both research and teaching it is important for US trained and China trained economists to work with one another because they have much to learn from one another.

In the development of economics education and research, China is not as advanced as in some other areas such as the export of industrial products. However, the leadership role China will play will be coming. Innovations will come when there are intelligent and able people working on a stimulating environment.

CHAPTER 15

Important Lessons from Studying the Chinese Economy

In 1979 the United States and China established normal diplomatic relations, allowing me to visit China and study the Chinese economy. After doing so for thirty years since advising the government of Taiwan in the 1960s and the 1970s and the government of the People's Republic of China in the 1980s and the 1990s, this is an opportune moment for me to summarize the important lessons that I have learned. The lessons will be summarized in four parts: economic science, formulating economic policy and providing economic advice, the special characteristics of the Chinese economy and the experience of China's economic reform.

To start off I should comment on the quality of Chinese official data on which almost all quantitative studies referred to in this article were based. Chow (2006) has presented the view that by and large the official data are useful and fairly accurate. The main justification is that every time I tested an economic hypothesis or estimated an economic relation using the official data the result confirmed the well-established economic theory. It would be a miracle if I had the power to make the Chinese official statisticians fabricate data to support my hypotheses. Besides, most of the data were published years ago before I conceived the ideas of the studies reported in this article.

15.1. On Economic Science

15.1.1. *The basic theories of microeconomics, macroeconomics and financial economics apply to China*

One should start with this proposition as a premise when studying the Chinese economy, but should be aware that there may be institutional differences that make it invalid. If by basic theory we mean not only the particular hypotheses presented in economics textbooks but the set of analytical tools we use in economics, then the applicability is broader.

Examples of the applicability of the theory of consumer demand drawn from my own studies include the estimation of total expenditure elasticities of demand for four categories of consumption goods in Chow (1985, Chapter 5; 2007, Chapter 9), studies of the demand for and supply of urban housing in China in Chow and Niu (2010), of demand for education in Chow and Shen (2006), and the demand and supply of healthcare in Chow (2009). All these studies confirm the basic theory, with estimated elasticities having the correct sign and a reasonable order of magnitude.

An example of applying the method of constrained maximization to explain behavior of state-owned enterprises in both the period of central economic planning and the period of the earlier years of economic reform is given in Chow (2007, Chapter 15). The first model constructed for the planning period assumes an objective function of the enterprise to be a function of total output and leisure time of the manager. Leisure time is defined as total time minus the time devoted to management and the time devoted to negotiations to obtain the required inputs used in production. The second model constructed for the early years of economic reform assumes an objective function which has profits and leisure time of the management as arguments. The reason for changing the model for this period is that the institutions were changed. State enterprises were allowed to purchase inputs in the market, thus making the use of the manager's time to negotiate for inputs unnecessary. They were also able to maximize profit which is the difference between revenue and the cost of inputs. When economic theory is applied the models may be different from those used to explain Western market institutions, but the basic tools of microeconomics, constrained maximization in this case, still apply.

The prices of stocks traded in the Shanghai Stock Exchange can be explained by the present value theory of stock prices, as reported in Chow (1999) and Chow (2007, Chapter 14) where panel data regressions (in log-linear form) of stock prices of different firms in 1992–1998 were performed on their dividends and rates of growth of dividends and the regressions can explain the Chinese data well. The values of the estimated parameters, when compared with those obtained from data of the New York Stock Exchange and the Hong Kong Stock Exchange, were similar in magnitude and reflected institutional differences in a reasonable manner, as explained in Chow (2007, Chapter 14).

Examples in macroeconomics include a study of inflation with the ratio of money supply to real output as the major determinant and formulated as an error correction model to describe the delayed effects is given in Chow (1987). The proposition of Milton Friedman on the effect of a monetary shock on output and prices, namely that the former effect is almost immediate but short-lived and that the latter effect is delayed but long lasting, is found to be valid in Chow and Shen (2005) using a VAR with log output, log price level and log money stock as the three variables. Both of these studies are summarized in Chow (2007, Chapter 7).

A simple macroeconomic model for China consisting of a consumption function and an investment function was presented in Chow (1987) and later updated in Chow (2009c). The consumption function is based on the permanent income hypothesis of Hall (1978), implying that consumption is a random walk. The investment function follows the principle of accelerations, with investment dependent on the rate of change, rather than the level of output and lagged investment. This model is found to well explain Chinese annual data since 1952.

A study of economic growth in China since 1952 by the use of a Cobb-Douglas production function was first presented in Chow (1993) and later updated as described in Chow (2007, Chapter 5). More on this study below.

15.1.2. *Market economy can work under different institutional arrangements*

Laws of economics apply to market economies of a variety of institutional arrangements. The different institutions include the extent to which a Western-style legal system is in place as compared with the use of moral codes and a system of social network and personal connections to guide business conduct in China, known as *guanxi*.

For example the economically efficient township and village enterprises flourishing in the 1980s and early 1990s behaved like private enterprises in a Western market economy as described in Chow (2007, Chapter 16). Secondly, the financial crisis of the Asian economies of 1997–1998 as described in Chow (2007, Chapter 4) can be explained by the same theories as for a financial crisis in a Western market economy. There is no need to appeal to "phony capitalism" to describe Asian market economies just because they are non-Western.

15.1.3. *Economic development can occur under different forms of government*

The Chinese economy has experienced rapid growth in a political environment different from those in Western democratic countries. Taiwan also experienced rapid economic growth from the 1960s to the 1980s under a government controlled by only one party. Before 1997 Hong Kong's market economy performed beautifully while being ruled by a government in London and not a democratic government of its own.

15.1.4. *Importance of human capital in economic development*

The quality of human capital, that is, the thinking, habit and skill of the population, is a major factor determining whether a developing country can develop rapidly. The other two major determining factors are the existence of a set of functioning (though possibly imperfect) market institutions and being in an early stage of development which allows the country to adopt the most advanced technology to catch up. My favorite evidence to support this point is the rapid economic growth of Germany and Japan after World War II when the physical capital of both countries were destroyed by the war but both countries had an abundance of high-quality human capital.

China happened to have an abundance of high-quality human capital in the form of skills of its workers and resourcefulness of its entrepreneurs and researchers, all having a habit of working hard. Such human capital was derived from China's cultural tradition of thousands of years. Different countries have different kinds of human capital. Some are more conducive to economic development than others. A part of the cultural tradition of China and other countries manifests itself in family education which may be more important than schooling in determining the human capital imbedded in a person and in a society. Different provinces in China have different potential for economic development just as different less developed countries may have different qualities of human capital affecting their development. The qualities of human capital may be related to geographical diversities, with good climatic conditions being favorable to the development of high-quality human capital.

15.1.5. *Economic forecast possible because of validity of econometric models and parameter stability*

Econometric models based on a sound economic theory are useful to provide accurate forecasts for the Chinese economy as well. One example is the forecasting of the overheating of the Chinese macroeconomy in 2004 and inflation in later years due to monetary shocks resulting from an inflow of foreign exchange as China had a large trade surplus. I made such a forecast in a speech given in the Bank of China in Beijing in 2005. Other examples include the accurate forecast of China's inflation in 1985 when money supply increased by 50% in 1984 as described in Chow (1994, p. 94) and the forecast of China's economic growth given in Chow (2007, Chapter 5).

15.1.6. *Forecasting institutional changes possible by using a similar methodology*

This topic is discussed in Chow (2007, concluding chapter, sections 2 and 3). The methodology is qualitative but similar in nature and steps as used to perform econometric forecasts in capturing the most important factors and their interactions and in the use of judgment to determine whether these factors will continue to operate in the future. The three examples that I cited were the predictions that economic reform would start after the disaster of the Cultural Revolution, that economic reform would succeed and that the Chinese economy would continue to grow for a long time. I predicted the continuation of rapid economic growth for China in publications through the late 1980s and the 1990s, including in particular in Chow (1989; 1994, Chapter 6). My prediction on China's economic development has remained unchanged since then. My simple working hypothesis underlying such a prediction is that the three fundamental engines for rapid growth, namely, high quality and abundance of human capital, a set of functioning market institutions and the early stage of development that allows China to catch up rapidly still prevail in China today, if we consider the less developed western provinces in China which still have room to develop.

Another example is the prediction that Hong Kong would remain essentially the same after its return to China in 1997, or return to China in 1997 would not affect Hong Kong's way of life. I made this prediction in the late 1980s based on my understanding of the Chinese government through years of working relationship. I invested in Hong Kong stocks at the time when the Hang Seng Index was about 2000 and the Index went up to more than five times soon after the change in government because the behavior of the Chinese government in relation to Hong Kong was just as I had predicted. If this example is not convincing, let me suggest that this prediction is analogous to investing successfully in the stock of a company in a given industry based on knowledge of the quality of its management, which may be based on the predictor's personal relation or friendship with its Chairman and CEO. A more convincing example is that a professor can use his knowledge of a graduate student to predict how successful she will be as a scholar in the future. A more systematic method for prediction based on qualitative knowledge was pointed out in the last paragraph. Needless to say, predictions based on qualitative knowledge are subject to error just as predictions based on quantitative knowledge by the use of econometric methods are subject to error.

15.2. On Economic Policy and Economic Advice

This section draws from Chow (2008) discussing the steps or gaps between acquiring knowledge from economic research to learning how to give economic advice, up to the point of affecting changes in the society.

15.2.1. *A gap between academic knowledge and ability to apply it for solving practical problems*

First-class academic economists have failed to see what parts of economics to apply in making suitable policy recommendations. They recognize this point when they start serving as adviser in government positions, as many American academics do by taking leave of absence to work in the government. They can testify that they have learned to provide policy advice through experience. The inability of macroeconomists in general to give policy advice without practical experience is analogous to the inability of microeconomic theorists to serve as CEOs of major corporations.

Besides the understanding of economics, other qualifications are required to give policy advice. First is the ability to recognize which part of economic knowledge is relevant for application to the given practical economic problem. A doctor who is trained in medical science may not always give the right treatment to a patient because he fails to recognize the nature of the patient's illness. It has been suggested that renowned economists at the International Monetary Fund failed to diagnose the problems for some economies including Indonesia in particular during the Asian Financial Crisis of 1997–1999. When the problem was a lack of liquidity, the policy recommended was to introduce discipline to government spending, which was just opposite to what the situation required.

As an academic economist with a full professorship rank in the 1960s, I did not know how to apply economic knowledge to solve economic problems until I began advising the government of Taiwan in 1967 as a young member of a team led by the late T. C. Liu and S. C. Tsiang and appointed by President Chiang Kai-shek.

I began to realize that when a practical economic problem appeared it was not easy to decide what economic tools should be applied. It was through practical experience in Taiwan that I first learned how to apply economic knowledge to solve real life problems.

15.2.2. *A gap between choosing the right economic knowledge for application and making a sound policy recommendation*

A good policy recommendation does not automatically follow the recognition and choice of a relevant economic theory. The recognition is necessary but not sufficient. Following is an example from my experience working with China's State Commission for Reconstructing the Economic System — the Economic Reform Commission in the 1980s. The Commission was chaired by the Premier, Zhao Ziyang to signal the importance of its work, although the meetings were usually chaired by Vice Chairman An Ziwen. A major issue was reform of the price system towards being market determined. Here we knew the problem was that certain prices were set too low as judged by the conditions of market demand and supply. The Economic Reform Commission was able to provide an excellent solution, the two-tier price system. In the case of residential housing, the existing tenants were given the right to stay in their apartments at low rents while commercial housing was allowed to be built and sold or rented at higher market prices. Those who could afford to pay for commercial housing were welcome to enjoy it. This solution to the housing problem was a Pareto improvement since no one was worse off, and some people became better off in living in better and more expensive commercial housing. A second example was the pricing of raw materials supplied to state enterprises. Such materials were available at market prices for additional inputs needed beyond the amount supplied by government channels at below-market prices. A third example is the swap center in Shanghai where importers and exporters could trade foreign exchange at a market rate which was higher for US dollars than the official exchange rate. The center provided foreign exchange when needed.

For readers who think that the above policy was based on such a simple idea that any practicing economist could have thought of it, they should recall the experience of the former Soviet Union and some Eastern European economies. These economies adopted a reform strategy of "shock treatment" by decontrolling prices overnight and by privatizing a large number of state enterprises within some five hundred days in the case of the former Soviet Union. This policy led to collapse in industrial production when state-owned enterprises were sold hastily to opportunistic investors who did not intend to manage them but purchased them at very low prices for resale. In adopting shock treatment as the policy for economic reform, the governments of these countries were following the advice of some well-known American economists who understood the virtues of a market economy. This case illustrates that have sound knowledge of economics does not guarantee having a good sense in providing sound advice on economic policy.

15.2.3. *Important points in giving economic advice*

First, consider the feasibility of the policy. One should not give any advice which is not politically feasible to achieve. Economists with their set ideals are often emotionally involved and cannot refrain from advocating them even when the ideal recommendations have no chance of being adopted. When they sell their impractical ideas to responsible government officials, they may even loose the latter's confidence, making it more difficult to give their advice later even when it becomes feasible.

Second, choose the right government officials to work with. This choice requires good judgment. If a potential adviser knows that the important officials cannot understand or appreciate her viewpoint she should not attempt to advise them. To force good ideas on the wrong persons would be counterproductive and would not lead to fruitful results. By a right government official I mean one who can understand the virtue of your recommendation and also has enough power to adopt a good proposal as government policy. I have met top government leaders who are not forceful enough to push through good ideas into government policy. Having the trust of such leaders is useless in affecting social change.

Third, choose the right time even if a potential advisor has found government officials intelligent enough to appreciate her ideas. If the advisor tries to push her ideas at the wrong moment, she will not find receptive ears and obtain a favorable response.

Fourth, an adviser needs to be open-minded and to recognize the possibility that she might be wrong. My own experience in working with members of the Economic Reform Commission in China has taught me important lessons about economics in action. I have learned as much for them as they might have learned from me. That is why interactive discussion to search for appropriate economic policies is a good strategy to follow.

In Taiwan in the 1970s, I was a member of the team of five economists advising the Taiwan government. We held discussions with the "Working Group of Five" at the time, consisting of the Governor of the Central Bank, the Minister of Economic Affairs, the Minister of Finance, the Director General of Budget, Accounting and Statistics and the Secretary of the Executive Yuan (branch of government). They were the government officials responsible for formulating and carrying out major economic policies at the time. In many a summers, we sat around an oval shaped table, with these five sitting opposite to five advisers from abroad. We met for one whole week in the mornings from nine to twelve. Each minister in turn would bring up his current economic problems for discussion while we listened, made comments and asked clarifying questions. After the first week, we went back to our offices to think, to discuss among ourselves and to do research on possible solutions to the problems presented to us. Six to eight weeks later the two groups met again. We presented our initial recommendations while they made comments and raised questions before a final draft of our recommendations was written up. The final draft was published in newspapers and became an important document having substantial impact on economic policy.

Serious discussions also took place with the same intensity in may meetings with members of the Economic Reform Commission of the

PRC. We met each time for about four to five consecutive days from nine to five. I invited selected members of the Taiwan team, in so far as possible, to participate in the meetings as well. By the 1980s T. C. Liu had already passed away and S. C. Tsiang was still a top economic adviser to the government in Taiwan and it was not convenient for him to take part, but I succeeded in inviting him in March 1989 to meet with members of the Economic Reform Commission including An Ziwen, Vice Chairman of the Reform Commission, and Liu Hongru, Deputy Governor of China's Central Bank (and an enthusiastic reader of Milton Friedman's work) by arranging the meeting in Hong Kong.

At that time, the most pressing economic issue for China was the control of inflation. Our solution, the tried and proven solution of S. C. Tsiang to cure the inflation in Taiwan in the 1950s, was to raise the interest rate to ensure a positive real return to bank deposits. The Commission adopted our recommendation and we were confident that it would work and it did. In sum, the open minded discussions with economic officials in both Taiwan and China mainland have taught me a great deal about economics in practice and provided me with a broad perspective required to solve real life economic problems.

15.2.4. *Using the framework of dynamic optimization to provide economic policy advice*

Section 1.5 has pointed out that econometric models are useful for forecasting in China. If so it should be useful in the formulation of good economic policies by setting the policy variables to achieve desirable targets for the variables of interest. The mathematical tool to achieve this, once an objective function of the variables of interest for a relevant time period in the future is given, is optimal control or dynamic optimization as presented in Chow (1975, 1997).

There was in the late 1970s a critique by Robert Lucas (1976) suggesting that the use of optimal control as a basis for economic policy advice was inappropriate, because the parameters of the econometric model would change as economic agents react to the policy or control rule of the government. Although many economists were persuaded by Lucas, others including Chris Sims (1980), Ray Fair (1984) and myself believed that his critique is invalid because the advice is not given in the form of a rigid rule that persists long enough for the economic agents to learn about and to react to. My explanation for the ready acceptance of the Lucas view by many economists is that by the middle 1970s econometricians in general had failed to build econometric models that were good enough to produce good forecasts. It was not difficult to build low-quality large-scale econometric models by extensive data mining, a practice which Ray Fair (1984) and Chow (1967) tried to avoid. Being disappointed by and having lost faith in the majority of econometric models, the profession readily accepted the Lucas critique, which also rode the waves of the adoption of the fashionable idea of "rational expectations."

Several considerations should be taken seriously in using the method of optimal control for economic policy recommendation. One should not simply and naively proceed to make policy recommendations in two steps: first, to find the optimal policy using an econometric model and second, to sell the policy to policy makers. It may be better to use the government official's objective function than to use our own objective function if we are to help the government official in making a best decision from his point of view. However, there is difficulty in achieving this, because not being technically equipped, a government official may not be able to communicate to us this objective function or be convinced that our recommendation will actually serve to achieve his objective.

A related point is that we need to acquire skill for explaining a result derived from the mathematics of dynamic optimization to a policy maker using a plain language and providing a good intuition. Furthermore, the economic adviser has to be able to instill confidence on the part of policy makers by successful communications on less technical matters. Then when the time comes to communicate the results of technical analysis as obtained by dynamic optimization, the government official may be willing to be persuaded.

A better approach is to make available a collection of good policies rather than just a single optimum policy to recommend. The economist needs only to convince the government official to adopt just one of these policies. More importantly, after he has his set of good policies and is able to be persuasive, he should be open-minded enough to let the government officials influence him and teach him that there might be other policies than those in his collection. It was for both the economic adviser and the government officials to get together to work it out, as illustrated by my experience in working with government officials in Taiwan and in the PRC. Good policies can be and should be worked out cooperatively and interactively. In the case of economic advice to the Taiwan government, an econometric model originally built by T. C. Liu was used to forecast major economic variables for different macroeconomic policy options, and the econometric work was frequently done in the office of the Director General of Budget, Accounting and Statistics.

15.2.5. *Implementation of government policies*

As discussed in Chow (2009a) among the pressing problems arising from rural poverty in China today, the most serious is the mistreatment of Chinese farmers by local Communist Party officials who have control over the affairs of local villages. Land contracted to farmers is illegally taken by local officials for urban development without adequate compensation. There is a law that guarantees the right of the farmers to keep the land that is contracted to them but this law has often been violated, leading to fairly wide-spread but often unreported demonstrations and unrests by mistreated farmers. The central government can not uphold its policy to protect the farmers, because it can not control the local party officials.

In the case of healthcare as discussed in Chow (2009b), after the collapse of the Commune system that provided healthcare and other services, many rural residents now receive worse health care services than during the late 1970s. This is a major case of failure during the very successful economic reform process in China. In recent years, the central government has tried to institute a medical insurance system for all rural residents. The insurance costs 50 Yuan per person per year and the government is willing to pay 40 Yuan, equally divided between the central and the local government. However, many farmers still did not enroll in this insurance system as of the spring of 2007, mainly because they did not trust the government in actually paying for the insurance premium for their benefit or in delivering the services as promised to the insured.

Given the importance of implementation, I would suggest that before policy recommendations are made and perhaps even before research to support the policy is completed, problems of implementation should be taken into account. If one knows that a certain policy cannot be implemented, recommending it is useless. As I have suggested before, a policy has to be feasible for us to recommend it. A policy that has no chance of being successfully implemented should be treated as an infeasible policy.

It is equally important to consider the problem of policy implementation in the design of the policy itself. In Chow (2008b) I suggested that if a provincial governor fails to enforce central environmental policies for protecting the environment, he should be subject to severe punishment, including the loss of his governorship. While making this recommendation I realized that the central government might not have such a strong resolve to adopt this policy. However I considered this recommendation feasible as long as there is some chance for its adoption.

15.2.6. *Making social change without going through the government*

The discussion in this section so far has concentrated on influencing the government in order to make social changes. There are two other important channels through which social changes can take place.

A most important channel is through the market. Social changes are made in a market economy by the actions of many individuals who innovate and by the adoption of their innovations through the market. Many universities and major corporations engage in research and development, the results of which are sold to the market and some have changed the society significantly.

A second important point known to economists is well expressed by Keynes who pointed out that the world is influenced more by men of ideas than by politicians who often follow their ideas. Karl Marx had tremendous influence on many government officials for decades, whether his ideas were valid or not. My respected teacher Milton Friedman perhaps had more influence than any other economist during the second half of the 20th century on the functioning of the American economy and many other economies than top government officials. His research has made a tremendous impact on society, including particularly in the formulation of monetary policy, the use of vouchers for paying tuitions, and the respect of freedom to choose in many aspects of life. He accomplished this by writing, speaking (on TV or in person) and teaching students.

15.3. The Characteristics of China's Economy

I have discovered that the values of many parameters describing the Chinese economy can reveal its institution characteristics and that some of these parameters even remain constant before and after the economic reform was initiated in 1978.

When Chinese farm families were free to build houses in the land distributed to them under the household responsibility system, while the urban workers were provided subsidized housing in the early 1980s, the total expenditure elasticity of demand for housing and fuel for farmers was high, equal to 1.78 as compared with the median of about 0.8 for the many countries studied by Houthakker (1957). See Chow (2007, pp. 166 and169). The total expenditure elasticity of demand for clothing in the fashionable Shanghai was as high as 1.61 while that of Beijing was 1.33 in the early 1930s. See Chow (2007, p. 170).

In a study by Johnson and Chow (1997), when using the Mincer equation to explain log wage by log years of schooling, years of working experience, its square and dummy variables representing gender, minority ethnic group, and Communist Party membership using data for rural and urban population in China for the year 1987, the signs and magnitudes of all coefficients are correct and reasonable. The rate of returns to education for both urban and rural population were low, being 3.7% and 4.0% respectively. This result reflects the large fraction of the urban labor force working in state-owned enterprises and the income of farm families being only slightly affected by years of schooling in the period of study. Being female, being a member of a minority ethnic group (other than Han) and being a Communist Party member were found to have a significantly negative, negative and positive effect on wage respectively, except for Party membership for the rural sample which has a statistically insignificant effect.

It is quite amazing that the random walk hypothesis of Hall (1978) explains aggregate consumption and the accelerations principle explains aggregate investment in China during both the period of central planning and after economic reform. A macro model based on these two equations was found to fit Chinese annual data in the period 1952–1982 and also in the period 1979–2006. See Chow (2009c). It is equally amazing that the same error-correction model with stable parameters can explain Chinese inflations before and after economic reform and likewise for the same VAR model that confirms Friedman's proposition on the effects of monetary shocks on aggregate output and the price level from 1952 to the 2000s. See Chow (2007, Chapters 6 and 7).

In a study of China's economic growth using a Cobb-Douglas production function presented in Chow (1993) and updated in Chow (2007, Chapter 5), the elasticity of output with respect to capital is found to be about 0.6 and with respect to labor to be about 0.4. These elasticity estimates agree with the estimate of 0.4 for the labor share of output for Chinese farm families given by Buck (1930) and with the estimate of 0.6 for output elasticity with respect to capital found in Mankiw, Romer and Weil (1992). These estimates remain unchanged before and after economic reform, but the increase in total factor productivity was found to be zero in the period 1952–1979 and to equal about 2.8% per year after 1979.

Chow (2002a) and Chow and Lin (2002) found that a similar study for the Taiwan economy yields an output elasticity with respect to labor of about 0.4 in the 1950s as shown by the fraction of output distributed to labor. This fraction increased gradually to about 0.48 in thirty years.

15.4. China's Economic Transformation Process

15.4.1. *Gradualism works*

In the discussion of economic reform in formerly planned economies, much debate centers on the issue whether the reform process should be gradual or rapid, the latter being referred to as shock therapy. I would not claim that gradualism works better for all countries including those Eastern European countries and the former Soviet Union, since I have not studied these countries well enough to render an opinion. There is no doubt from my studies of the Chinese economy, however, that gradualism was the right policy and has worked for China's economic reform for the following reasons.

First, reform in China required receiving support from the Communist Party members to carry it out. It was impossible to tell the party members that a market economy was good after they had been told in no uncertain terms otherwise. It would take time and evidence to change their minds. Deng Xiaoping had the genius to advocate "seek truth from facts." This was to tell the Party members to respect evidence rather than ideology. An experiment was carried out in 1979 to give two thousand selected state enterprises more autonomy in decision making in the production of outputs. Foreign investment was first introduced in special economic zones, etc. All of these took time.

Secondly, the Party leadership did not have a blueprint for reform because they simply did not know what market institutions to adopt although they had learned that the existing planning system did not work through years of experience. They required time and experimentation to find the workable market institutions.

Third is the institutional inertia imbedded in entitlements provided to the state enterprises and the population. Urban population receiving housing subsidies in the form of very low rent of several yuan per month could not accept price reform that could raise the price by a substantial amount. Reform of prices had to proceed gradually.

More on these points is found in Chow (2007, Chapters 3 and 4).

15.4.2. *Allowing both state sector and non-state sector to co-exist and compete*

A slow reform process means that many state run institutions would remain inefficient for a long time. To speed up economic growth, which is required to give reform momentum and support, the policy was to allow the non-state sectors to flourish and serve as an engine for growth. An example was the growth of the township and village enterprises. Even Deng did not expect the sudden appearance of these enterprises. Appropriate economic institutions would naturally appear and flourish, and they did in China, once opportunity was given.

15.4.3. *Use of dual price system*

An institution supporting the coexistence of state and non-state enterprises is the dual price system as mentioned above. The state enterprises could obtain raw material from the state distribution channels at a below-market price as before but only for a fixed amount. In the mean time they could obtain the material in the market at a higher price. Since this fixed subsidy does not affect the optimum input and output decisions, the state enterprises could still behave optimally. The same dual price system applied to urban housing when higher priced housing was available in the market, and to the supply of foreign exchange when a foreign exchange swap center enabled the importers and exporters to trade foreign exchange at a market price.

15.4.4. *Economic liberation through the open-door policy*

Foreign trade and foreign investment, as well as travel abroad, were allowed, enabling the free flows of goods, capital, technology and people. This increased efficiency in the allocation of resources and helped speeding economic growth. China also improved its management skill and technology in the process, while the state enterprises became more efficient from competition of imports and of foreign owned enterprises. China has for years had an export surplus and accumulated a large amount of foreign reserves, over 2 trillion as of

April 2009. It has begun investing overseas as it emerges as an outward looking economy. In terms of its total output measured in purchasing power parity terms China is already a great economic power, second only to the US.

However, China's economic liberalization process is gradual and cautious. In foreign trade, the exchange rate is not entirely market determined. Foreign investment has been subject to regulations. So are the banking and financial sectors. Derivative products in financial markets are introduced gradually. Consumers learn to use credit cards step by step. All these slow movements have protected China from much of the current financial crisis and economic slowdown in many parts of the world and enable China to play an important role in leading the world economy to recovery.

Studying the Chinese economy can help one become a better economist and may even be useful for improving the economic institutions of the world.

References

Buck, John L. (1930). *Chinese Farm Economy*. Chicago: The University of Chicago Press.

Chow, Gregory C. (1967). "Multiplier, accelerator and liquidity preference in the determination of national income in the United States." *Review of Economics and Statistics*. XLIV, pp. 1–15.

Chow, Gregory C. (1975). *Analysis and Control of Dynamic Economic Systems*. New York: John Wiley.

Chow, Gregory C. (1985a). *The Chinese Economy*. New York: Harper and Row.

Chow, Gregory C. (1985b). "A model of Chinese national income determination." *Journal of Political Economy*, 93: 782–792.

Chow, Gregory C. (1987). "Money and price level determination in China." *Journal of Comparative Economics*, 11: 319–333.

Chow, Gregory C. (1989, September 27). "Prospects of China's economic growth, foreign economic relations and cultural exchanges with the U.S." *Princeton Alumni Weekly*, pp. 16–17.

Chow, Gregory C. (1991, March 27). "The Chinese economy: Substantial growth in the 1990s." Presented at the Mid-Pacific Conference on the

Evolving Pacific Basin: Problems and Opportunities for Trade and Investment. *Commercial Times.* [Taiwan], p. 2.

Chow, Gregory C. (1993). "Capital formation and economic growth in China." *The Quarterly Journal of Economics*, 108: 809–842.

Chow, Gregory C. (1994). *Understanding China's Economy.* Singapore: World Scientific.

Chow, Gregory C. (1997a). *Dynamic Economics: Optimization by the Lagrange Method.* New York: Oxford University Press.

Chow, Gregory C. (1997b). "Challenges of China's economic system for economic theory." *American Economic Review*, 87: 321–327.

Chow, Gregory C. (1999). "Shanghai stock prices as determined by the present value model." *Journal of Comparative Economics*, 553–561.

Chow, Gregory C. and Anloh Lin. (2002, September). "Accounting for economic growth in taiwan and Mainland China: A comparative analysis." *Journal of Comparative Economics*, 507–530.

Chow, Gregory C. (2002a). "Taiwan's aggregate production function and economic growth." In Sheng-Cheng Hu and Chu-Tan Fu, ed. *Essay on Economic Development in Memory of Academician Hsing Mo-huan.* Taipei: Institute of Economics, Academia Siknica, 21–43.

Chow, Gregory C. (2002b). "Can economists forecast accurately?" A keynote address presented at the meeting of Academia Sinica in Taipei, July 1 2002. *International Chinese Statistical Association Bulletin*, July 2003, 28–36.

Chow, Gregory C. and Yan Shen. (2005). "Money, price level and output in the Chinese macro-economy." *Asia-Pacific Journal of Accounting and Economics*, 12, 91–111.

Chow, Gregory C. (2006, June) "Demand for education in China." *International Economic Journal*, 20:2, 129–147.

Chow, Gregory C. (2006, June). "Are Chinese official statistics reliable?" *CESifo Economic Studies.*

Chow, Gregory C. (2007). *China's Economic Transformation* (2nd ed.). Blackwell Publishers.

Chow, Gregory C. (2008a). "From research to social change." *Comparative Studies* (*Bijiao*, in Chinese). China Civic Press, issue 36, 24–33.

Chow, Gregory C. (2008b). "China's energy and environmental problems and policies." *Asia-Pacific Journal of Accounting and Economics*, 15, 55–70.

Chow, Gregory C. (2009a). "Rural poverty in China: Problem and solution." In Ravi Kanbur and Xiaobo Zhang, ed. *Governing Rapid Growth in China: Equity and Instituions.* New York: Routledge, 229–246.

Chow, Gregory C. (2009b). "An economic analysis of health care in china." In Gordon G. Liu, Shufang Zhang and Zongyi Zhang, ed. *Investing in Human Capital for Economic Development in China*. Singapore: World Scientific.

Chow, Gregory C. (2009c). "Note on a model of Chinese national income determination." *Economic Letters*. Available on line at http://dx.doi.org/10.1016/j.econlet.2009.11.018

Chow, Gregory C. and Linlin Niu. (2010). "Demand and supply for residential housing in urban China." In Joyce Man, ed. *China Housing Policy*. Cambridge, MA: Lincoln Institute Press.

Fair, Ray C. (1984). *Specification, Estimation and Testing of Macroeconomic Models*. Cambridge, MA: Harvard University Press.

Hall, Robert. E. (1978). "Stochastic implications of the life cycle-permanent income hypothesis." *Journal of Political Economy*, 86, 971–987.

Houthakker, H. S. (1957). "An international comparison of household expenditure patterns, commemorating the centenary of Engel's law." *Econometrica*, 25, 532–551.

Johnson, Emily and Gregory C Chow. (1997). "Rates of return to schooling in China." *Pacific Economic Review*, 2, 101–113.

Lucas, Robert. (1976). "Econometric model evaluation: A critique." In K. Brunner and A. H. Meltzer, ed. *The Philip Curve and Labor Markets*. Amsterdam: North Holland Publishing Company.

Sims, Christopher A. (1980). "Macroeconomics and reality." *Econometrica*, 48, 1–48.

CHAPTER 16

US Housing Bubble and Economic Downturn

The current economic downturn in the US has lasted longer than many people expected. There is little hope for the unemployment rate to reduce from the present 9.6% to below 8% within a year. The economic downturn started with a housing bubble. Housing prices first increased because financial institutions were able to make profits by packaging mortgages as securities for sale and the consumers were lured to buy houses with no down payment. When the prices of the securities and the houses went down, financial institutions incurred great losses and were unable to provide liquid funds for the producers and consumers to make their necessary purchases. Because of the collapse of financial institutions a serious economic recession followed. People became unemployed and could not afford to purchase consumer goods. Many home-owners cannot afford to continue their monthly payment to the bank which holds their mortgage loan. In 2010, 4.1 million home-owners, as compared with 3.1 million in 2009, are expected to give up title to their property as they cannot repay the outstanding mortgages. Of the 4.1 million, 3.5 million will be foreclosures and 600,000 will be short sales. A short sale occurs when the mortgage holders allow the owner to sell the property for less than the outstanding mortgages to avoid the cost of foreclosure, estimated to be about $75,000 per home. Given a total of 50 million homes with mortgages at the beginning of 2009, 3.1 and 4.1 million homeowners giving up title to their property are large numbers.

In China the market of urban housing, especially in some cities like Shanghai and Beijing, is extremely buoyant, with demand very high and prices increasing rapidly. China did not experience a housing bubble as in the US. It is unlikely that China will experience a housing bubble like the one in the US because the economic institutions are different. Chinese financial institutions are not allowed to take the kind of risks involved in packaging mortgages as securities as in the US. Chinese consumers are not allowed to purchase houses without sufficient down payment. The Chinese government is watching the market for urban housing carefully. It has introduced measures such as increasing the down payment for the purchase of a second home and taxing the resale of homes purchased within two years.

How did the American financial institutions and consumers get to the conditions they were in when the bubble started? Engaging in extremely risky investment in packaged securities by financial institutions and purchasing a house without putting in any down payment by consumers were not typical behavior in the United States two decades ago. There are a number of explanations for this change in behavior. Some said the government was to blame because it failed to regulate adequately the behavior of financial institutions including investment banks in particular. Through Fanny May it provided low cost mortgages to consumers. It failed to protect consumers adequately when they use credit to purchase an excessive amount of consumer goods that they cannot afford. Such alleged failures of the government have led to recent legislation and executive action to introduce new regulations for financial institutions and to set up a new agency for consumer protection. Others may say that the financial institutions and the consumers themselves are to blame. Whatever the cause of the recent economic downturn, corrective actions by the government would still be appropriate.

Whether such government actions are sufficient to prevent future financial crisis and the ensuing economic downturn is difficult to say. The Great Depression of the early 1930s led to changes in government policies in increasing government expenditures to make up for insufficient aggregate demand and the introduction of social security and unemployment insurances. The current serious economic downturn was caused by institutional failures that were not antici-pated by the preventive legislations of the 1930s. Accordingly one needs to be prepared for economic problems to occur in the future which are not expected today and cannot be fixed by the current legislation.

CHAPTER 17

Will Consumption Expenditures in China Increase Rapidly?

After the world economic downturn and the slowdown in the growth of Chinese exports, there has been concern in China that the steady growth of the economy will be affected. One proposed solution is for the government to encourage the increase in domestic consumption expenditures to make up for some of the loss in exports. In this article I would like to present some evidence to suggest that there may be a rapid increase in domestic consumption simply because the consumers themselves decide to do so.

I had a glimpse of this phenomenon when I travelled to Shanghai in July 2010. I saw enthusiastic buying in shopping malls all over the city by crowds of people. During a recent trip to Hong Kong in January 2011, I saw and heard about groups of consumers from China mainland simply purchase all the items in the store without asking for the prices. They asked for the most expensive items and told the store clerk to give them the entire stock available in the store. Some Hong Kong people criticized such mainland consumers and this kind of behavior became a common subject of conversation among local residents. Americans and Europeans have also observed the extravagant Chinese consumers in their countries. Of course these are examples of consumer behavior of the very wealthy. However, their behavior may affect the total consumption of the country because the poor may try to emulate the rich. This possibility remains to be investigated.

If such signs of rapid increase in consumption require an explanation, I would like to suggest the following. Economic changes can occur in discrete jumps after the process of change has continued for some time. An Example is change in fashion when all of a sudden consumers decide to buy a particular type of new clothes. In this example promotion and advertising by the producer of the new brand may have caused the rapid change but sometimes no special promotion has occurred. In the consumer markets after increases in the consumption of various categories of commodities and services, the consumers may suddenly change the style and composition of consumption. This could be occurring in China as the consumers are becoming richer and more sophisticated. Consumer purchasing behavior can change just like fashion in clothing can change suddenly. Once a large enough number of consumers in China decide to show off their wealth, the rest may try to follow to "keep up with the Joneses." There are also other explanations of the increase in consumption, such as by the behavior of the younger generations born after the one-child family policy was introduced in 1980 who are less thrifty than their parents and grand-parents.

An outside promoter can affect fashion. Similarly the Chinese government can affect and has affected total consumption in the Chinese economy, as the 12th Five-Year Plan singled out the promotion of domestic consumption as a main objective. There is sudden increase in travel as speedy highway and railroad transportation became available. This trend is noteworthy in view of the past concentration in production and exports. The Chinese are beginning to consume more and import more. The latest statistics in the month of February 2010 is that China imported more than it exported. A part of the increase in imports was for consumption.

As consumption becomes more varied and sophisticated we can expect that arts and music will be developed since these can be considered a part of consumption. Cultural activities are both consumption and investment in human capital. Decadence may also come with such activities if an observer tries to use his own judgment to decide what is good for the consumers . Those believing in "free to choose" will consider such activities a sign of progress for the Chinese society.

CHAPTER 18

From Guangzhou Opera House to Issues of Economic Development

Having grown up in Guangzhou and returning to visit frequently in the last thirty years, I was excited to read an article in the *New York Times* dated July 6 about the newly-built Guangzhou Opera House the among buildings that are less distinguished. That building alone improves the look of the city center tremendously. The article praises it as the "most alluring opera house built anywhere in the world in decades."

The Guangzhou City government deserves credit in selecting such an outstanding architect as Zaha Hadid of the UK to build this remarkable building. As I witness another significant event signaling the rapid development of the Chinese economy, I reflect on the lessons learned from observing the development process:

1. The success of economic development often depends on the performance of the best, rather than the average. Economic development is propelled by a few most talented people. As a country for visitors, China depends on a few most distinguished sights including Huangshan and Guilin. As a university town, Princeton is known for having the most distinguished scientist Albert Einstein. China's policy for economic development in the 1980s "to let some members of the society get rich first" was consistent with this view of economic development, so is the government policy of showcase projects.

2. Such a strategy for economic development, while correct and necessary, creates social problems of inequality and discontent. Such problems need to be solved. In China when the income of the urban population increased at a higher rate of some 7.5% annually as compared with the 5.5% for the rural population, there has been much discontent among the latter population.

3. Solutions to the social problems of inequality again depends on a few people. It is up to the top government officials to find ways to solve these problems including the provision of social welfare benefits for all in order to equalize consumption levels. At the same time the successful and the rich in the private sector also have a responsibility to share their wealth with the poor. In China charity is beginning to be practiced, as the economy becomes more developed.

4. The quality of development is uneven. Starting with the Guangzhou Opera House itself, there is no associated opera company as those in more developed economies, the performances are of poor quality and the construction work is poor in many places. As for the poor construction, many of the 75,000 exterior stone panels were so shoddily made that they are already being replaced. Some plasterwork in the lobbies looks as if it was done by an untrained worker who had never picked up a trowel before.For the city itself the architecture of the neighboring buildings is mostly poor. Now these building are mixed with a very outstanding one. Observers of China's economic development would express admiration and disappointment at the same time, as I have often heard from travelers to China in recent years.

The uneven quality can be improved if people responsible for such distinguished projects pay more attention to this problem. In the case of the Guangzhou Opera House, more experienced workers from Hong Kong could be hired to construct the more difficult part of the building and the best opera companies in the world can be invited to performed more frequently, for example. Of course all this will cost money but money is what China has. Such balanced strategy applies to large projects undertaken by the Chinese government as well.

For example, in the construction of high speed railroads, the quality of design, material and workmanship should all be considered. More broadly speaking, economic planning in China can be improved by considering the total economic effects of individual projects rather than just their immediate impacts.

CHAPTER 19

Lessons from the Current American Great Recession

The current American recession started four years ago with unemployment rate over 9% for over 27 months. Economists do not know when the economy will return to normal. There is much that we don't know about this recession. Hence there is much that we don't understand about the functioning of a market economy. However there are important lessons that we have already learned.

First, a market economy can have problems of a very serious recession. Many economists and the educated public once believed that from the lessons learned during and after the Great Depression of the early 1930s, we had found the cure for such a depression. Now we know that we have not found the ways to prevent or even to shorten a very serious recession. After the Great Depression Keynes wrote *The General Theory of Employment, Interest and Money* which claimed that by increasing government expending we can stop or at least slow down the economic downturn. At the end of WWII, Keynesian economists thought that because government expenditures on the war were to end there would be a recession but the recession did not occur. Post WWII economic prosperity generated doubts about the Keynesian theory of depression and might have helped promote the free market ideas of Milton Friedman. After examining the history of the Depression Friedman came to the conclusion that the Depression was not the result of malfunctioning of the free market but of mistaken monetary policy of the government. If the increase in money supply is maintained at a steady and modest rate there would not be a very serious recession. The last great recession has shown that Friedman was wrong also. Hence this great recession has taught us what we don't know, or what we thought we knew was incorrect.

Secondly, there is much in economics that we still know about allocation of resources not only in normal times but even when such a great recession occurs. When the relative price of a product goes up today, the demand will still decrease, for example. When income goes up, the demand for normal consumer goods would still increase. I have used such simple micro-economics to explain why the prices of urban housing in China increased so rapidly since the mid 1990s. The explanation is that urban income has increased rapidly, causing the demand for urban housing to increase. At the same time the supply of the total stock of urban housing which the consumers desire cannot keep up with demand. This explains why the price of urban housing relative to the general consumer price index has gone up so rapidly.

Third, globalization has not reached the stage where a great recession in one major country like the US can cause a serious economic slowdown in all other major countries. For China, demand for its exports to the US declined but real GDP in China continued to increase at over 9% per year since 2008. Neither was the high rate of growth of real GDP in India greatly affected.

Fourthly, for China which has experienced continued rapid economic growth, we should be aware of the possibility of a serious economic downturn in the future. This may not happen in the current decade but it may happen when the economy has become a more matured market economy. It is important for us to study the causes of the American recession and observe carefully the future recovery of the American economy as this may help us prevent serious fluctuations in our own economy. We should also observe carefully the changing institutions of our own economy and see if there are features of the institutions which are subject to extensive risk taking similar to those that have caused the current great American recession.

PART 3

Economic Policies

CHAPTER 20

How to Improve University Education in China?

The development of university education has been rapid in recent years. The number of graduates from institutions of higher learning increased from 848 thousand in 1999 to 5.31 million in 2009. The quality of higher education has also improved. Can the quality improve even faster in the future? What can be done to improve higher education?

In studying economic reform we have observed the improvement in the production of goods and services by state and non-state enterprises. The main principles underlying market reform of state enterprises are to allow them to make their own decisions and to allow all enterprises to compete. These basic principles apply to universities which produce educational services. They are practiced in other countries today and were successfully practiced in China before the introduction of Soviet style central planning in 1953. They are now practiced in China for the primary and secondary schools to a large extent. The tight control of universities was introduced by the need for central planning but this need has disappeared when we decided to have a market economy.

On the principle of allowing decentralized decision making in the management of university education, the following contrast with the management of enterprises can be observed:

University administrators are not given freedom in the same way as managers of state-owned enterprises to act to the best interests of the students and the faculty and to promote education as they see fit. They are restricted by the rules set by or the need for approval by the Ministry of Education in (1) Freedom to allocate funds available for different purposes. (2) Lack of freedom to determine size of student body in different areas, such as the number of MBA students. (3) Freedom to determine the size of the faculty and staff and the sizes and locations of physical facilities. Freedom to allocate human, physical and financial resources for different purposes is basic to the proper functioning of any management. (University administrators in Hong Kong are subject to similar restrictions to some extent.) The main reason for giving autonomy to the university administrators is that they know the conditions facing the university better, and ways to serve the interests of the students and the faculty and staff better than someone higher up and further away in the Ministry of Education.

For the university students let me mention: (1) Freedom to choose a major only after completing one or two years of college education. (2) Freedom to choose more electives to broaden one's education. (3) More time for independent thinking and less time in attending classes. To set quotas for students majoring in different fields was necessary during the period of economic planning because production targets of various kinds were set and people with specified training in different fields were required to produce the goods specified. Now the market decides what to produce and the people choose their education, their profession and their job. Demand and supply should determine the numbers of students majoring in different fields.

For faculty members let me mention: (1) Freedom to travel to professional meetings or to do research abroad without approval by the Ministry of Education. (2) Freedom to visit other universities in China mainland, Hong Kong and Taiwan provided that a suitable hosting institution can be found. Approval by the chairman of his department or the dean of his school would be desirable because the former has the responsibility to offer courses to students and cannot allow too many faculty members to be absent at the same time.

Now I turn to competition among universities. To what extent can the tuition be set by the universities? There should be no fear that if given this freedom some universities will overcharge the students because competing universities will try to attract the best students by offering the best quality of education at the lowest cost. Faculty members should be allowed to relocate freely just as blue and white collar workers can choose their employers. This would allow each professor to work where his services are most highly valued. He would be able to choose the best environment for his professional development and his ability would be best utilized for education and research.

Some people in China may still be influenced by the ideas prevailing during the period of central planning before 1978 and do not fully understand the successful working of the forces of demand and supply after market reform in improving the provision of other goods and services in the Chinese economy. In the case of higher education, autonomous universities, just like autonomous state or non-state enterprises, can best decide the kind of educational services to provide and how to provide them. The choice of the consumers will insure that the services provided are worthwhile. No doubt some universities may have lower standards than others, but they provide services to students who may have lower qualifications. In this regard, one should not criticize easily the schools run separately by an established school on the side because their existence shows that there is demand for their services. Without them the students could not receive an education. People usually know the quality of such schools and what a diploma from each school is worth.

Policy for education in China is a complicated subject. This paper deals only with university education. Even for university education, it does not discuss university education policy in general and what the important responsibilities the Ministry of Education should have. It only suggests that autonomy be given to universities in the same way that autonomy is given to state enterprises.

Once the contrast between this outdated policy for higher education and the corresponding successful policy for state enterprises is clear to the government leaders, I expect that autonomy of universities for the betterment of higher education will be forthcoming in the current enlightened environment of China's successful economic development.

CHAPTER 21

How to Manage a University Well?

In the last chapter I discussed how to improve Chinese universities by providing them with sufficient autonomy. In this chapter I would like to discuss how to manage a university well.

In the early 1980s a delegation of university presidents from China came to visit Princeton University to find out what education system it has to make it such a great university. I suggested to them that the high quality of Princeton depends on having a first-rate faculty. Without such distinguished faculty members a Chinese university cannot learn from Princeton University documents on ways to make his university as good. This article starts with the premise that the quality of a university is measured by the quality of its faculty. Hence, the main responsibility of a President is to provide a good environment for its existing faculty to pursue teaching and research and to recruit good new faculty members to do the same.

There are two approaches to achieve this. The first is by central direction, and the second is by decentralized decision making. Since the faculty members themselves know the best what the most suitable environment is for teaching students and conducting research and who the best new faculty members are, their opinions have to be respected and considered seriously by the president in decisions on these matters. The president should also note that the faculty members may have self-interests which are not consistent

with the interest of the university. For example a mediocre department will tend to recruit new faculty members that are also
mediocre. The faculty members should be consulted but the
President should use his judgment to filter the recommendations
from the faculty.

There is one important issue concerning the administration of a
department. The principle that the faculty's opinion counts implies
that the department that represents them counts. But how should
the department be administered, by a chairman with great authority
or by a chairman with limited authority? The authority of the chairmanship varies somewhat from university to university and from
departments to departments at the same university, but the important point is that from the university point of view each department
should be given sufficient autonomy because the faculty members are
the key players. University presidents can commit and have committed mistakes by centralizing decision making, i.e., by delegating
responsibilities to university administrators to oversee matters that
are best left to the discretion of individual departments or individual
faculty members.

The mistakes in centralizing decision making are often made at
the beginning of a presidency when a new president wishes to impose
his ideas and make a mark on the university before understanding the
culture of the university that has been shaped by its faculty for years.
I have witnessed a number of instances of such mistakes in universities in the US and in Hong Kong. A president who understands that
the faculty members are the key players is less likely to make such a
mistake.

The topic of this article is how to manage a university and not
what makes for a good president of a university. The latter topic
will cover at least two characteristics, vision and personality. A president with vision should and will decide what new directions the
university should be heading, for example, the development of a
new field or a new school, with proper consultation with the faculty
of course. Another good quality of a good president outside the scope

of this article is the personality that makes the faculty members feel at home and being a part of a family. Such a quality applies to the chairman of a department and to the dean of a school. I have admired some of my colleagues in certain US, Hong Kong and Chinese universities who have such a quality which I myself do not possess.

CHAPTER 22

How to Improve the Efficiency of State Enterprises?

It is well-known that during the period of central planning, state-owned enterprises were inefficient and their employees provided poor services to customers. There was no incentive to serve the customers well in retail stores, restaurants, hotels, banks and ticket counters for theatres and bus and railroad stations. Some public officials even derived satisfaction from creating inconvenience to the people they served because when they needed the services of other officials they were similarly treated. If productive efficiency is defined as the ratio of output to input and if the quantity of output of a service is adjusted for the quality of the service, then improving the quality of service mentioned above amounts to improving the efficiency of state enterprises. This essay will suggest possible actions by the National Development and Reform Commission and by the National People's Congress to solve the problem.

This kind of behavior gradually disappeared in private and other profit seeking enterprises after economic reform towards a market economy, but it still persists in most state-owned enterprises today. Recently I encountered two interesting instances of such behavior. The first appeared in Xiamen when my tennis coach of Xiamen University took me for a tennis lesson in a tennis court owned by the City of Xiamen. We tried to pay for the use of the court but were told to go to the next building to purchase a card required to make the payment. When we tried to purchase the card, the computer system was not working and we had to wait for someone to come to repair it. We wanted to leave the required payment to the employee and obtain permission to play before the computer was to be fixed. If either the card issuer or the tennis court attendant had agreed we would have been able to use the court, but both refused. There were three empty tennis courts in front of us! My coach took me to another place to play.

Later I speculated what would have happened if we had simply walked into a court to play. Would the court attendant have called the police to chase us out? If so the police should side with us because the tennis courts are public asset belonging to the citizens of Xiamen and my coach as a citizen had the right to use them. It was the negligence of the attendant who failed to perform his duty as a keeper of this public asset to serve the public. My coach told me that the last time he used those courts they were operated by a private enterprise and the service was good but the City government took it back after seeing the profitable operation.

The second incident occurred in a branch office of the Bank of China in Beijing. I opened a savings and a connected checking account in 2008 and obtained a debit card that required a password. Later I went to the Bank to find out my password because I had forgotten it. I had to wait for about 20 minutes before being served. The teller told me that I had to open a new checking account with a new password. (Looking back perhaps I should have challenged his statement and asked to talk to the manager, but I did not.) No matter whether the statement was a rule of the Bank of China or an irresponsible response, it represented an inefficiency of the operation of the Bank. It took me about 40 minutes to complete opening the new checking account by filling out a new application form and repeatedly entering my password some 12 times while waiting for the teller to fill out several other forms required. Finally the teller told me that my new account was opened and gave me a new debit card. When I tried to use the card the next day and afterwards I was told each time that my account did not have sufficient fund to pay, not even for breakfast for two persons in my hotel, when I knew I had much more! What would have happened to me if I had to depend on my deposit in the Bank of China to pay for expenses during this trip?

These two incidences are examples of what commonly occur every day in China as inconveniences of daily life. Economic inefficiency and poor service of state-owned enterprises were subjects discussed in my book *China's Economic Transformation* (Chinese edition, Remin U Press, 2005). I related by experience of staying in a poorly operated Dongfang Hotel in Guangzhou in 1980 but discovered that it was efficiently operated with very good services and restaurants in 1987 when a new Hong Kong operated China Hotel was across the street and when the management of Dongfang received reward for running a profitable operation. Hence I discovered that a state-owned enterprise can be efficient if the management is rewarded for making profits and if there is competition from other enterprises, private or public.

If we were able to reduce the ordinary inconveniences of everyday life, not only would the Chinese people be happier, but the entire economy would operate more efficiently. One simple solution to reduce such annoyances and more importantly to increase overall economic efficiency in China is to transfer the ownership of state-owned enterprises to private ownership or to private operation through a leasing arrangement as much as possible and to allow and foster competition in areas where the state-owned enterprises operate, as I have discussed in my book *China's Economic Transformation*. Given that such methods to improve the efficiency of state enterprises are available, perhaps the National Development and Reform Commission of China can set up a study group to survey all such reform possibilities nationwide and introduce reforms in all cases discovered by the methods as suggested. This would increase the rate of economic growth of China and make China a more harmonious society where people can live more happily.

State enterprises are public assets. Under public ownership Chinese citizens are the owners of the public assets. However, in practice the civil servants who are assigned the duty to manage public assets often fail to perform their duty as in the case of the two persons managing the public tennis courts in Xiamen. More serious cases of mismanagement of public assets are committed by public officials who receive bribes or transfer public funds to their personal accounts as custodians of public assets. These are cases of corruption punishable by law. In the first case of this essay the civil servants managing a public asset did not try to take any bribe. They simply failed to perform their duty. Chinese citizens who are victimized by such failures should be protected by law. They should have the right to sue these civil servants for failure to manage the public assets properly. If I ask someone to manage my apartment and he fails to manage it properly I have the right to sue him for mismanagement. Public assets belong to the citizens. The citizens as owners have the right to sue the civil servants managing these assets for mismanagement. The Chinese People's Congress can enact a law to make such a violation of the right of the citizens illegal and punishable by law.

I presented this essay on June 29, 2010 before a seminar for faculty and graduate students in the Shanghai University of Finance and Economics and would like to acknowledge with thanks the helpful comments from the participants of the seminar without implying that they necessarily agree with the views expressed.

CHAPTER 23

Carry Out the Open Door Policy Further

To carry out the open door policy further is an important objective of the Chinese government. Recently I was impressed by an example of this policy in Southwest University of Finance and Economics (SWUFE) which appointed a distinguished American professor Phil Dybvig as Dean of Institute of Finance. There are examples on deans of schools of economics or finance who are full time professors of American universities but they are all Chinese. The above is the first example of a non-Chinese being appointed dean of a major Chinese university that I know of. I was very impressed by this example and wondered what the vast pool of talents would be if other universities follow this example.

Later it occurred to me that when I was a freshman in Lingnan University in Guangzhou in 1947 there were American professors, department chairmen and deans. Lingnan University was founded by Americans in 1888 and its Presidency was transferred to a Chinese educator Zhong Yongguang in 1923, but many American professors and chairmen of departments remained. During the period of central economic planning China closed its door. All private universities including Lingnan were closed in 1952. It was leader Deng Xiaoping who initiated economic reform towards a market oriented economy in 1978 that had led to the rapid economic development in China. Realizing the success of the open-door policy present-day Chinese leaders continued the policy and extended it further.

As in many other aspects of China's economic reform, leadership of the Central government not only initiated and directed reforms but allowed and encouraged local governments and lower-level units to take actions as they saw fit. The example of SWUFE mentioned above is a case in point. Imagine what will happen if other universities follow this example, not only in finance and economics but in other fields including natural sciences, mathematics, engineering and medicine. The talents available to China are unlimited.

CHAPTER 24

How to Stop Inflation in China?

Today China is having inflation. Most recently the State Council sent orders to provincial and city governments to control prices. Generally speaking, the use of price control is not an effective way to control inflation. Recall that in 1961, during the period of central planning, China had price control but the retail price index went up by 16.2% according to *China Statistical Yearbook*. The main reason for inflation is the rapid increase in money supply relative to real GDP. In 1961, real GDP was reduced by 30%. To slow down inflation the basic solution is to reduce the rate of increase in money supply.

In April 14, 2010 I wrote an article in China Business News entitled: Can inflation be avoided? That article gave statistical evidence from 1952 to 2009 to support my theory that inflation in China is determined by three important variables. The variables are the change in the ratio of money supply to real GDP, inflation of the last year and the deviation of the price level in the last year from its equilibrium relation with the ratio of money supply to real GDP. From this statistical relation that I estimated, I projected inflation in 2010 if money supply were allowed to increase. My conclusion was, "The current policy of the People's Bank to slow down the increase in money supply has been correct and the Bank needs to continue to restrict the increase in M/Y in order to maintain a stable price level."

As reported by Reuters on Sept 11 from Beijing, the annual growth in China's broad M2 measure of money supply was 19.2% in August compared with 17.6% in July and well above forecast of 17.5%, the People's Bank of China said on Saturday. Money supply as measured by M2 increased by 29.7%, 27.7%, 26.0% and 19.2% (as compared with a year ago) respectively in Nov 2009, Dec 2009, Jan 2009 and Aug 2010. Realizing the inflationary pressure generated by such large increases in money supply, the People's Bank began in April 2010 to increase the interest rates and raise the reserve requirement for commercial banks several times but failed to slow down the increase of M2 to a satisfactory level.

It is understood that the main reason for the increase in money supply outside the control of the People's Bank is the inflow of foreign exchange which is converted to RMB. The reason for the inflow of foreign exchange has been the foreign trade surplus generated by the undervaluation of the RMB. The basic solution to the inflation problem is therefore the revaluation of the RMB to a substantially higher level to eliminate the trade surplus. This may require an increase of some 20% or perhaps an even larger amount.

The Chinese government has not raised the exchange rate of RMB substantially mainly because of the possible disadvantages of doing so. The main disadvantage is the reduction of certain exports which helped generate output and employment in China. However, such disadvantages are outweighed by the many advantages. There are two major advantages. The first is to solve the inflation problem as we have discussed. The inflation problem may be more serious in the future if money supply is not controlled properly. The second is to allow China to import more in the future at lower prices (since the Chinese currency will have a higher value as compared with foreign currencies). This will allow China to buy more for domestic consumption and for capital formation to speed up economic growth. Because of the undervaluation of the RMB China has had trade surplus for many years and has accumulated over 3 trillion US dollar worth of foreign exchange reserves. This amount of hard-earned money is not effectively utilized because much of it has remained idle and a substantial amount is invested in US Treasury bonds yielding a low rate of interest.

Since it is to China's advantage to increase the exchange rate of RMB substantially, I hope that the government will have the determination to undertake this important measure in spite of opposition from some domestic interest groups.

CHAPTER 25

How to Solve the Problems of China's Inflation and the American Recession?

In Chapter 24 I suggested raising the exchange rate of the RMB to solve the problem of inflation in China. In Chapter 16, I explained the American problem of housing bubble and economic recession. In this chapter I suggest a way to help solve both problems.

First I suggested to stop inflation by raising the exchange rate of the RMB. Raising the exchange rate of the RMB will stop the trade surplus of China and slow down the inflow of foreign exchange. The inflow of foreign exchange is the main course of increase in money supply that has caused inflation in China.

A policy to support the revaluation of the RMB and to slow down the net inflow of foreign exchange is to draw down or to spend the 3 trillion dollars of foreign reserves that China has. This would increase the supply of foreign reserves, especially the US dollar, in the market where Chinese and US currencies are traded and thus lower the value of the dollar relative to the value of the RMB. China's foreign reserves can be used for many important purposes. I suggested using it for the strategy of Western development. In the 12th Five-Year Plan there are many important projects that can be financed by using our foreign reserves. The government can decide which project to be financed in this way and by how much.

How would the spending of foreign reserves help solve the problem of the American recession? In the United States, there is a high rate of unemployment. The rate remained as high as 9.6% for many months before it was even increased further to 9.8% as reported at the beginning of December 2010. The Federal Reserve in early November increased money supply by 400 billion dollars with the purpose of stimulating economic activities but was criticized by some respected economists who said that this policy was bad because it increased the debt of the American government. Too much government debt will lower the credibility of the US government and make it difficult to borrow the future. Increasing money supply will also cause inflation in the US in the future.

If China uses its foreign reserves to purchase American goods, it will increase aggregate demand in the US and thus help the American economy to recovery from its current serious recession. The US government and the American people have criticized China for taking away jobs from the US. They said that imports from China replaced American goods that are domestically produced and led to lower production and higher unemployment in the US. The policy of buying American goods as suggested will have the opposite effects. Buying American goods by using China's foreign reserves will also reduce the debt of the US government because much of China's foreign reserves is held in the form of US Treasury Bonds.

Although China's policy on setting the exchange rate of the RMB is based on its domestic economic considerations the American government and people have criticized the Chinese government for maintaining a low exchange rate of the RMB in order to create an export surplus of China and thus harm the US. Once China raises its exchange rate such an unreasonable criticism will disappear.

For all the reasons stated above, the relation between China and the US will be improved by the policy of using up China's foreign reserves to purchase American goods in carrying out important strategies under the 12th Five Year Plan. This policy is a win-win policy for China.

CHAPTER 26

China's Aging Population

The aging population of China is an obvious phenomenon, as can be seen by the chart on the change of China's population by age groups. The ratio of population aged 50 or over to population 20–49 was $148/400 = 0.37$ in 1980, increased to $350/670 = 0.52$ in 2010 and is expected to increase to $526/600 = 0.88$ in 2025. The reason for the increase is the decline of the number of young children aged 4 and below after 1980. We need more young people to grow up to become productive members of the society.

Note that demographers today can predict the numbers of people in age groups 20 and over in 2030 very well, because these people are already born and how many in each age group will survive can be accurately predicted. It is harder to predict the number of people in age groups below 20 in 2030 because these people are not yet born but demographers can use the numbers of women in child bearing ages together with China's population policy to form a good prediction because these women are already born.

Although the source of this chart is slightly over 10 years old with data after 1995 being projected figures, the chart serves to show the main point about an aging population in China. A reader disagreeing with the right-hand side of the chart displayed can replace it by his own without affecting the major statements of this article that China's population is aging and the only way to slow it down is to encourage a higher birth rate for the population. By finding a more recent chart a reader can also find out how accurate the prediction of the chart based on the research of the United Nations Population Division was.

Population growth in China by selected age groups

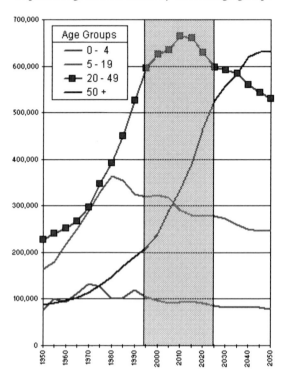

Source: United Nations Population Division (1999): World Population Prospects. The 1998 Revision. New York (Data on Diskettes).*

Because of the population policy introduced in 1980, China has relatively many more old people today as compared with 30 years ago. The aging process will continue in the next two decades. It is not my purpose to discuss the economic and social consequences of our aging population. We all agree that serious problems associated with an aging population exists in China. The solution is to allow a higher birth-rate so that the fractions of young people in the population will increase.

---

*The chart can be found in the website: http://www.iiasa.ac.at/Research/SRD/ChinaFood/data/pop/pop_1.htm.

CHAPTER 27

China's Environmental Policy:
A Critical Survey

For over three decades China has achieved remarkable success in economic development unmatched in human history. Such a rapid economic development has naturally carried with it considerable damage to the natural environment.

The environmental problems facing China in the course of its economic development were serious. To illustrate, according to a 1998 report of the World Health Organization (WHO), of the ten most polluted cities in the world, seven were found in China. Air pollution was caused by coal combustion that generated sulfur dioxide and soot as two major air pollutants, resulting in the formation of acid rain falling on about 30% of China's total land area. Industrial boilers and furnaces consume almost half of China's coal and are the largest sources of urban air pollution. The burning of coal for cooking and heating, in many cities, accounts for the rest. Serious water pollution was caused by coal-fired power plants that released mercury into the air later captured by raindrops, and transferred to surface water and groundwater. China's water is polluted also by the disposal of waste. Water beds of several important cities including Beijing and Shanghai are low, causing shortage of supply of well water. Supply of waters from rivers including the Yellow River and the Yangtze River are running short because of diversion to agriculture production and electricity generation along the sources.

Against this background, the Chinese government has been formulating its environmental policies. Ever since the beginning of economic reform initiated in the late 1970s, the government has paid serious attention to environmental problems. It is neccessary to survey the basic laws and policies of the Chinese government on environmental problems, the degree of success in policy implementation, the prospect of solving the environmental problems in the long run and some recent successes in the development of alternative energy and in controlling pollution. In addition two proposals for improving the regulation of industrial pollution in China and for controlling carbon emission in the world will be suggested.

27.1. Laws and Basic Policies

The 2010 World Expo in Shanghai was a show case of the importance that the Chinese government treated the environmental problem, not only in the construction of the facilities for the Expo and of the Chinese Pavalion itself, but also in the pronouncements that have been made by the government on its attention to the protection of the environment.

The Chinese central government has been aware of the environmental problems and has made serious attempts to protect and improve China's environment. As early as 1979, China passed the Environmental Protection Law for trial implementation. The 1982 Constitution included important environmental protection provisions. Article 26 of the Constitution requires that "the state protects and improves the environment in which people live and the ecological environment. It prevents and controls pollution and other public hazards." There are also provisions in the Constitution on the state's duty to conserve natural resources and wildlife. Based on these provisions a number of special laws have been enacted. These include the Water Pollution Prevention and Control Law of 1984, the Air Pollution Prevention and Control Law of 1987, the Water and Soil Conservation Law of 1991, the Solid Waste Law of 1995, the Energy Conservation Law of 1997 and several important international agreements including the Kyoto and Montreal Protocols. In June 2002, China enacted the Cleaner Production Promotion Law, which established demonstration programs for pollution regulation in ten major Chinese cities, and designated several river valleys as priority areas.

The State Environmental Protection Administration (SEPA) was established in 1998 to disseminate national environmental policy and regulations, collect data and provide technological advice to the State Council on both national and international environmental issues. SEPA was elevated to become the Ministry of Environmental Protection in the Spring of 2008 to emphasize its importance and to give it more power on policy for CO_2 emission, China appears to be more concerned with the problems of air and water pollution since the CO_2 emission problem is less urgent for China. President Hu Jintao stated on Thursday, June 7, 2007, during the G8 meetings in Germany the principle of "common but differentiated responsibilities" for developing countries in tackling climate change. "We should work together to make sure the international community upholds the goals and framework established in the United Nations Framework Convention on Climate Change and its Kyoto Protocol (in 1997)" while developing countries should also carry out "active, practical and effective cooperation… Considering both historical responsibility and current capability, developed countries should take the lead in reducing carbon emission and help developing countries adapt to climate change… For developing countries, achieving economic growth and improving the lives of our people are top priorities. At the same time, we also need to make every effort to pursue sustainable development in accordance with our national conditions."

At the UN sponsored conference on climate change in Copenhagen in January 2009, Premier Wen Jiabao stated that China was determined to do its share but would not subject itself to international inspection, a position opposed by the United States. From the economic point of view, the protection of environment can be treated as the government's attempt to correct a major market failure. The failure occurs when natural resources available in the environment are underpriced and over utilized because users of resources like air and water often do not pay for the cost of using it. However, the role of the Chinese government is broader in scope than simply correcting this market failure. In the Chinese planning system guided by the National Development and Reform Commission targets are set up to reduce the energy/output ratio and the emission/energy ratio.

For example on Friday, May 8, 2007, Premier Wen Jiabao made a speech stating that the current macro-control policy must focus on energy conservation and emission reduction in order to develop the economy while protecting the environment. The Chinese government had set a target in the 11th Five-Year Plan of reducing energy consumption for every 10,000 yuan of GDP by 20% by 2010 (or 4% per year), while pollutant discharge (presumably measured by an index of quantities of different pollutants) should drop by 10%. The National Development and Reform Commission have also set targets for carbon emission.

27.2. Two Kinds of Policy: Regulation and Control vs. Economic Incentives

From the analytical point of view we can divide the policies for environmental protection into two kinds. The first kind is command and control. For example the US government has specified Corporate Average Fuel Efficiency (CAFE) standards for automobiles sold in 1978 and 2007. For the promotion of the use of alternative technology to produce energy, the government can specify a given share of electricity to be produced by renewable resources. The second kind is to provide economic incentives to save energy or to reduce pollution. An outstanding example is to tax the use of gasoline. Another is to require emitters to pay for permits according to the amount of emission. The permits can be traded among polluters. This is known as a cap and trade scheme.

So far in China the laws are mainly of the regulation and control variety rather than market-based policies, partly because the government has not been able to design a set of appropriate market-based policies, e.g. to estimate the appropriate tax rate. However there have been attempts to experiment with such policies. For example, there was an agreement in a December 11–12, 2007 cabinet level economic strategy meeting with the US for the two countries to cooperate in introducing emission permits and other economic incentive schemes for controlling pollution. A system of emissions trading for sulfur dioxide, similar to that used in the United States, is being tested in some cites with pilot projects, and may eventually be applied nationwide. The Chinese government will also advance reforms in the pricing of natural gas, water and other resources, raise the tax levied on pollutant discharge, establish a "polluter pays" system and severely punish those who violate the environmental protection laws. Future Chinese environmental initiatives may also include formulating a tax structure beneficial to environmental protection, and granting preferential loans and subsidies to enterprises that construct and operate pollution treatment facilities. The government will also provide incentives to companies that use more energy efficient production facilities and techniques. In recent years China has succeeded in promoting the use of alternative energy and in reducing pollution as will be discussed below.

On March 10, 2010 the National Development and Reform Commission (NDRC) disclosed that it was formulating guidelines for the development of low-carbon economy, and that small scale carbon trading pilot programs will be launched in specific industries and regions. To achieve the target of reducing global green house gas emissions by 50% by 2050, investment in low-carbon technologies between 2005 and 2050 will total 1.2 trillion US dollars. China vowed to reduce the intensity of carbon dioxide emissions per unit of GDP in 2020 by 40–45% compared with the level of 2005 at the Copenhagen conference.

27.3. Problem of Enforcement

Although the laws to protect the environment appear well conceived in general and the government has set up an administrative structure for environmental protection, there have been serious failures for central government to achieve its environmental policy objectives. A main reason for the failure is that local governments interested in economic development of their region do not cooperate. It is often to the advantage of local governments to allow pollution to take place illegally in order to promote a higher rate of economic growth and the central government cannot control them. Local government officials benefit from higher levels of output in their region as they receive credits for economic development and sometimes bribes from polluting producers. Given the Chinese system of public land ownership stated in the Constitution, rent seeking local bureaucrats who control the use of land have the tendency to approve the use of land for urban development during their term of office. This has led to overdevelopment of land from the viewpoint of its optimal utilization in the long run and was often an important cause of overheating of the macroeconomy, besides creating environmental problems.

In recent years the Central government recognized this problem and changed its policy for evaluating the performance of local government officials to include the record on environmental protection. The National People's Congress enacted on October 28, 2007 a Law on Conserving Energy by stating that work carried out by local government officials in energy conservation should be integrated into the assessment of their political performance along side with output growth. Such efforts have yielded positive results as will be discussed below.

As an example of failure to meet targets to protect the environment, in April 2007 Premier Wen stated: "The challenge of reducing energy consumption and greenhouse gas emissions has proved arduous as China's economy grew 11.1% in the first quarter (of 2007) but power consumption surged 14.9% ... Energy consumption as a fraction of GDP fell only 1.23% in 2006, well short of the annual goal of 4% (as stated in the 11th Five-Year Plan of 2006–2010)."

In the long-run, however, there are reasons for expecting improvement in the implementation of China's environmental policies for three reasons.

1. The strong resolve of the central government as already discussed.

2. The central government has the power to enforce such laws because the operation of an industrial enterprise requires its approval and sometimes even its assistance in the provision of land or credit. In

order to protect and improve the environment the government not only can punish the offender but can provide economic incentives for people to act for the economic welfare of the society.

3. There will be a strong positive income effect on the demand for a clean environment. As the Chinese economy gets more developed the demand for cleaner water and air will increase, and the Chinese people can afford to pay for it. In the long run, though not necessarily in the near future, this favorable income effect should more than offset the unfavorable effect of producing a large quantity of output as the experience of the developed economies has demonstrated. The early increase in pollution followed by a reduction in a later stage in the course of economic development is known as the environmental Kuznets curve. This inverted U shape in the relation between pollution and per capita income is expected to take effect in China in the future.

27.4. Recent Successes in Promoting Alternative Energy and in Controlling Pollution

According to the *New York Times*, August 25, 2009, although solar energy remains far more expensive to generate than energy from coal, oil, natural gas or even wind, the global economic downturn and a decline in European subsidies to buy panels have lowered its price.

Chinese companies have played a leading role in reducing the price of solar panels by almost half over the previous year. Production of solar panels have increased because production cost in China is lower than in other countries and, since March 2009, the Chinese central and local government have provided heavy subsidies to solar panel manufacturers, including free land, and cash for research and development. State-owned banks are flooding the industry with loans at considerably lower interest rates than available in Europe or the United States.

The largest company, Suntech in Wuxi, has become the second largest manufacturer in the world, second only to First Solar of the United States. Many firms in China have entered the market. Some are planning to produce in the US to avoid American protectionist policies against imports from China. Although the production of solar power is increasing, it remains a very small source of energy, with an expected total capacity in 2020 (20,000 megawatts) equal to only half of the output of coal-power plants built in one year.

The successful development of solar panels shows that the Chinese government is capable of identifying an important product to subsidize in order to promote its production for the purpose of economic development and that the Chinese entrepreneurs are ready to take advantage of the government subsidies and the favorable production and marketing conditions in China to expand the production and export of this product. The government's success in promoting the production of clean energy is not limited to solar panels. China has doubled its total wind energy capacity in each of the four years between 2006 and 2009, and was expected to pass the United States in 2009 as the world's largest market for wind power equipment. China is also building considerably more nuclear power plants than the rest of the world combined, and these do not emit carbon dioxide after they are built.

Secondly a success story in the control of air pollution by the use of SO_2 scrubbers is reported in a PhD thesis by Xu Yuan (徐袁) at the Woodrow Wilson School of Public and International Affairs of Princeton University. In the 10th Five-Year Plan (2001–2005), China's SO_2 emissions went up by 28% and missed seriously the goal of reducing emission by 10%. However, in the 11th Five-Year Plan (2006–2010), the trend has been reversed. In 2008, China achieved a 9% reduction of SO_2 emissions from the 2005 level, almost reaching the goal of 10% by 2010. The most dramatic change happened at coal power plants: China managed to install SO_2 scrubbers at both newly built coal power plants and old ones as retrofits. At the end of 2008, China had 363 GWe of SO_2 scrubbers, or 60% of the total capacity of coal power generation (601 GWe). By comparison, the ratio at the end of 2005 was only 10%.

The achievement came from the central government's effort in mobilizing both the leaders of local governments and managers of coal power plants. For the former, two measures were taken in the 11th Five-Year Plan: (1) promotion and removal of leaders according to the success in the operation of SO_2 scrubbers. (2) using the power to suspend construction of large projects which may affect the environment (including new coal power plants over 200 MWe) since by law large construction projects require ratification by Ministry of Environmental Protection according to its assessment of the environmental impact of the project. To increase the capacity of supervision by site visits, the total personnel at all government levels increased from 37,934 in 2001 to 52,845 in 2006, or by 39.3%.

In providing incentives to managers of power plants, the most important policy in the 11th Five-Year Plan for the operation of SO_2 scrubbers is called "desulfurized electricity price premium": After installing SO_2 scrubber, a coal power plant is allowed to sell its electricity to the electric grid at a price 15 RMB/MWh higher than the original price, if the SO_2 scrubber is under normal operation; it would be fined 75 RMB/MWh if its SO_2 scrubber were shut down. Although many coal power plants with SO_2 scrubbers were receiving the price premium as early as 2004, the penalty and other detailed regulations were not enforced until July 2007.

What are the reasons for success in the control of SO_2 emission? Will the same reasons work for controlling air pollution in China in general? There are two conditions favorable for the success in the use of SO_2 scrubbers. First, the source of pollution, namely coal power plants, is easy to identify and control. Second, the method of solution by the use of scrubbers is clear cut. Hence it is easy to design policies for the local government officials and for the plant managers to follow. Other cases of air pollution by consumers and by other industrial producers may be more difficult to identify and the methods of solution may not be as straight forward. However, the success in the case of SO_2 scrubbers has demonstrated the resolve and the ability of the central government in controlling air pollution. And we can expect that the government will try to deal with more difficult cases even if the effort may be less successful and more time consuming.

It has been the policy of the Chinese government to promote the development and use of clean energy and to prevent economic production from polluting the environment. I have just cited one successful example in carrying out each of these two policies.

While teaching a graduate course on the economic analysis of environmental problems at the Hong Kong University of Science and Technology in the Spring of 2010, I asked the students to provide examples of successful policies in protecting the environment and in the promoting of clean energy. Some of these examples are cited in the Appendix.

27.5. Proposals for Regulating China's Industrial Air Pollution and for Controlling World Carbon Emission

On the protection of China's environment and the control of carbon emission in the world, many useful ideas are being put forward for the consideration of the Chinese government.

Here I cite two examples of my own. First, to improve the regulation of industrial air pollution in China the proposal consists of the following components.

1. Industrial polluters will have to pay for pollution permits issued by the local office of China's Environmental Protection Administration. Any amount of pollution by a polluter, however small, requires having a permit to pollute or emit that amount. The proceeds from the permits will be returned to the local Chinese citizens in some appropriate manner. The number of permits issued (total amount of pollutants discharged) will be determined after consultations with representatives of the local citizens who will be affected by the pollution. The citizens and their representatives presumably balance the harm and benefit of pollution in their area under this proposal.

2. Given the number of permits issued, demand will determine the price per permit. The government will first set an initial price for polluters to purchase the permits. If the price is lower than the equilibrium price, the permits will run out and some polluters need to

purchase them from others. If the initial price is too high, there will be unsold permits which the government can sell to late comers at a price lower than the initial price until all permits are sold.

3. Local officers of the State Environmental Administration receive directions from local Chinese citizens through their representatives. Residents in rural areas can be represented by the popularly elected village heads. Urban residents can be represented by their popularly elected representatives of the locality. These representatives will be given responsibility to determine and will have incentive to enforce policies to protect the environment.

This proposal echoes two major policy objectives of the Chinese government in economic development, (1) market reform and (2) promotion of a democratic government. Under the proposal market oriented policies to regulate air and water pollution would be formulated democratically. Citizens would participate in the formulation of environmental policies and would thus help to enforce them, rather than protesting against too much pollution as many have done in recent years.

In the implementation of this policy there might be difficulty in monitoring the amount of pollution emitted. This difficulty can be resolved by requiring the polluting factories themselves to submit amount of emission, with false reporting subject to heavy penalty. There might also be inertia on the part of government officials to adopt such a policy as there would be for other policy proposals. Strong resolve on the part of the leaders in the central government would be required for this policy to be adopted even if they are convinced of its merits.

I wrote a letter to Premier Wen Jiabao about this proposal and he suggested a Vice Minister in the Ministry of Environmental Protection to meet with me in Beijing in July 2008 to discuss it. I met with him and several accompanying staff members. The meeting was cordial and friendly and the idea was passed onto these officials for their possible consideration. The control of industrial pollution is a complicated matter. There are other considerations that the officials have to take into account which I may not be aware of.

The second proposal is to regulate carbon emission through a UN resolution. It consists of the following components.

1. The total amount of CO_2 emission in the world is decided as the median of amounts submitted as votes by members of the General Assembly. The median rather than the mean amount would be adopted in order to prevent any member nation from submitting an extreme value to affect the outcome.

2. All countries are required to have permits for the emission of CO_2 not to exceed the amount specified by the permits.

3. Permits are issued by the UN in proportion to size of population under the principle that each world citizen has an equal right to use the atmosphere which is a natural resource. Emitting CO_2 in the atmosphere is an act of utilization of this resource.

4. Emission permits can be traded between any two countries at prices mutually agreed upon. It is expected that developing countries like China with low level of CO_2 emission per capita will obtain financial gain by selling permits. Developed countries like the United States which emit a large amount of CO_2 per capita will need to buy permits. Buying permits is an equitable way for the US to finance the effort of developing countries in limiting CO_2 emission as it has expressed its willingness to do.

China may be attracted by this proposal to make clear to the world that it is not emitting an unduly large share of carbon and that it is willing to play its role in the control of total carbon emission in the world.

Appendix

Examples of Policies for the Development of Clean Energy and the Control of Pollution in China cited by Hong Kong University of Science and Technology students

A. *Development of Clean Energy*

In the 11th Five-Year Plan, China decides to increase greatly the production of biomass energy, the supply of electricity from the burning of municipal solid waste and agricultural waste through the construction of power plants to burn these fuels, and to expand the production of solid biomass, bio-ethanol and bio-diesel. It includes targets to achieve 5 million kw of grid inter-connected wind power and 5.5 million kw of grid inter-connected electricity from biomass combustion.

Current efforts to offset coal consumption include the development of natural gas and coal-bed methane infrastructure, increasing the number of combined heat and power plants, adding approximately 3000 megawatts (MW) of hydropower annually, and developing renewable energy resources such as wind and photovoltaics for electricity generation.

For China's electricity generation, renewable sources of energy (including hydroelectricity) accounted for 18.6% in 2001, second to coal. With assistance from the United Nations and the United States, China hopes to embark on a multi-million dollar renewable energy strategy to combat pollution.

China has established a National Working Group for Dealing with Climate Change (国家应对气候变化策略小组) since 1990, and the group became National Leading Group for Dealing with Climate Change (国家应对气候变化领导小组) directed by the Premier in 2007. This group has been devoted to fostering the Clean Development Mechanism (CDM), which specially emphasizes the utilization of renewable energy under an emission trade framework.

China has made a great effort on hydropower. The construction of the Three Gorges Dam started on 1994 and is expected to be fully operated around 2011. It is the world largest hydroelectric power station. According to BP Statistical Review — Full Report 2009, the annual hydroelectric energy produced in China in 2008 was 585.2TWh.

According to China's National Climate Change Program, China is promoting the development of bio-energy. There were more than 17 million household biogas digesters that generate 6500 million cubic meters of biogas annually. The installed capacity of biomass generation is about 2 GW, among which sugar-cane fired power capacity is about 1.7 GW and landfill-powered 0.2 GW. Production capacity of ethanol fuel based on crops was 1.02 million tons.

The Ministry of Agriculture encourages the use of marsh gas in rural areas. The government also encourages the production of alcohol from various plants and the use of alcohol for energy.

One provision in China's Renewable Energy Law of 2006 encourages continued wind development. It requires power grid companies to buy all output of local registered renewable energy producers and aims for 70% of China's wind turbines to be produced locally. Provincial governments have also incorporated targets for wind power generation capacity in their five-year plans.

China is currently developing carbon capture and storage facilities for its coal plants. In Nov 2009, US and China established a renewable energy partnership. Besides the bio-fuel, solar and wind technologies to be developed, the two countries will also focus on modernizing the electrical grid with new transmission lines and smart grid technology. From 2001 Dongfeng Automobile Co. was asked to develop a new type of electric bus for the Beijing 2008 Olympics. The company worked really hard on this project.

Although it failed to carry out a perfect production due to the speed problem and only 40 of their buses were used during the Olympics, the new technology was applicable for family-size vehicles. The remaining problem is to reduce the cost of production.

In the development of natural gas, a number of LNG (Liquefied Natural Gas) stations have been built. The government is also planning to increase nature gas import and building many LNG receiver stations around the coastline. LNG application courses are held at the universities.

B. *Environmental Protection*

The Chinese government has succeeded in forbidding the use of plastic bags. Now China is consuming and producing hundreds of billions fewer plastic bags, with many women taking a cloth bag for shopping.

PART 4

Quantitative Economic Studies

CHAPTER 28

Note on a Model of Chinese National Income Determination*

A macroeconomic model of Chow (1985) explaining aggregate consumption by the permanent income hypothesis of Robert Hall and aggregate investment by the accelerations principle was found to fit Chinese annual data from 1952 to 1982 well. This note shows that the same model can successfully explain Chinese annual data from 1978 to 2006.

The model of Chow (1985) starts with the national income identity $Y_t = C_t + I_t$ where Y_t, C_t, and I_t denote respectively national income, consumption and investment in year t in constant prices. $X_t =$ exports − imports is omitted as a component of Y_t, because during the sample period 1952–1982 this variable is less than half of one percent of Y, except for 1982 when it equals 1.6%.

Consumption C is determined by the permanent income hypothesis of Hall (1978), namely, as a random walk with drift. To determine investment I assume that desired capital stock K* equals a constant plus aY, and that actual change in capital stock $K_t - K_{t-1}$ equals a fraction b of the desired change in capital stock or $b(K_t^* - K_{t-1})$. Substituting the linear function of Y for K* in this equation and solving for K_t give $K_t = \text{const.} + abY_t + (1 - b) K_{t-1}$. Since gross investment I_t is defined as $K_t - (1 - d)K_{t-1}$ where d is the annual rate of depreciation, we can subtract $(1 - d)$ times the

* Originally published in *Economic Letters*, 106 (2010), 195–196.

equation for K_{t-1} from the above equation for K_t to obtain an equation for investment

$$I_t = K_t - (1 - d) K_{t-1} = \text{const.} + ab[Y_t - (1 - d)Y_{t-1}] + (1 - b)I_{t-1}.$$

Given a small rate of depreciation which is equal to about 0.04 for the capital stock in China, investment I_t depends on the rate of change in output Y according to the accelerations principle.

I have estimated this same model using Chinese data from 1978 to 2006. Data on Y = GDP, C, I and X = exports − imports (measured in 100 million RMB) in nominal terms are presented in Table 1. To obtain these variables in constant prices I have divided them by a price index. The price index, also presented in Table 1, is the ratio of Y in nominal terms to Y in real terms. The consumption and investment equations are estimated by the method of two-stage least squares. In the first stage Y_t is estimated by a regression on C_{t-1}, I_{t-1}, X_t and X_{t-1} to yield, with X assumed to be exogenous,

$$Y_t^* = 140.8(116.4) + 0.8841(0.0604)C_{t-1} + 1.4254(0.0951)I_{t-1}$$
$$- 0.4815(0.2616)X_t + 1.4073(0.2883)X_{t-1}$$
$$R^2 = 0.9996; s = 273.4. \tag{1}$$

The number in parentheses after each coefficient is its standard error. The variables are measured in 100 million RMB in 1978 prices, with the price index in 2006 equal to 4.598 as shown in Table 1.

In the second stage of two-stage least squares I have estimated the consumption function

$$C_t = 218.86 + 1.067(0.074) C_{t-1} - 0.0051(0.0371)Y_t^*$$
$$R^2 = 0.9985; s = 271.24. \tag{2a}$$

This result confirms the permanent income hypothesis of Hall perfectly since the coefficient of C_{t-1} is almost exactly 1 and the coefficient of income Y is almost equal to 0. Given the result (2a) I have dropped the variable Y_t^* and re-estimated the consumption function to obtain

$$C_t = 226.05(91.78) + 1.0570(0.0079) C_{t-1}$$
$$R^2 = 0.9985; s = 266.08. \tag{2}$$

Table 1. Data on China's National Income and Its Determinants.

Year	Y	C	I	X	P
1978	3605.6	2239.1	1377.9	−11.4	1
1979	4092.6	2633.7	1478.9	−20	1.054896
1980	4592.9	3007.9	1599.7	−14.7	1.098124
1981	5008.8	3361.5	1630.2	17.1	1.137733
1982	5590	3714.8	1784.2	91	1.164813
1983	6216.2	4126.4	2039	50.8	1.168049
1984	7362.7	4846.3	2515.1	1.3	1.201187
1985	9076.7	5986.3	3457.5	−367.1	1.305023
1986	10508.5	6821.8	3941.9	−255.2	1.387854
1987	12277.4	7804.6	4462	10.8	1.453304
1988	15388.6	9839.5	5700.2	−151.1	1.63712
1989	17311.3	11164.2	6332.7	−185.6	1.769711
1990	19347.8	12090.5	6747	510.3	1.904878
1991	22577.4	14091.9	7868	617.5	2.035682
1992	27565.2	17203.3	10086.3	275.6	2.175614
1993	36938.1	21899.9	15717.7	−679.5	2.558603
1994	50217.4	29242.2	20341.1	634.1	3.075886
1995	63216.9	36748.2	25470.1	998.6	3.490539
1996	74163.6	43919.5	28784.9	1459.2	3.722223
1997	81658.5	48140.6	29968	3549.9	3.750238
1998	86531.6	51588.2	31314.2	3629.2	3.685385
1999	91125	55636.9	32951.5	2536.6	3.605819
2000	98749	61516	34842.8	2390.2	3.604115
2001	108972.4	66878.3	39769.4	2324.7	3.672308
2002	120350.3	71691.2	45565	3094.1	3.717834
2003	136398.8	77449.5	55963	2986.3	3.829693
2004	160280.4	87032.9	69168.4	4079.1	4.088025
2005	188692.1	97822.7	80646.3	10223.1	4.358183
2006	221170.5	110413.2	94103.2	16654.1	4.598263

Sources: Y = GDP, C = Consumption, I = Investment, X = exports − imports in nominal terms, measured in 100 million RMB, are found in Tables 3–15 of *China Statistical Yearbook 2007*. The price index P is the ratio of Y in nominal terms and Y in real terms, the latter given in Tables 3 and 4 of *China Statistical Yearbook 2007*.

The investment function is

$$I_t = -399.04(139.79) + 2.4149(0.6470)\ Y_t^* - 2.2861(0.6281)$$
$$Y_{t-1} + 0.2233(0.2369)I_{t-1}$$
$$R^2 = 0.9968;\ s = 327.4. \tag{3a}$$

Note that the coefficient of Y_{t-1} is opposite in sign and slightly less in magnitude (because of the rate of depreciation) to the coefficient of Y_t^*. This confirms the accelerations principle that investment depends on the rate of change in income.

Given the coefficients of Y_t^* and Y_{t-1} in Eq. (3a) to be almost equal in magnitude I replace these variables by the variable $(Y_t^* - Y_{t-1})$ to obtain the investment function

$$I_t = -186.23(120.84) + 1.7782(0.6513)(Y_t^* - Y_{t-1})$$
$$+ 0.6866(0.1589)I_{t-1}$$
$$R^2 = 0.9960;\ s = 359.28. \tag{3}$$

In Chow (1985) I reported results similar to Eqs. (2) and (3) obtained by using Chinese annual data from 1952 to 1982. In the consumption function the coefficient of lagged consumption was almost equal to 1 and the coefficient of income was 0. In the investment equation the coefficient of Y_{t-1} was negative and slightly less in magnitude than the coefficient of Y and I replaced these variables by their difference as in Eq. (3). The results showed that the coefficient of this difference in the investment equation was smaller than 1.7782 possibly because the ratio *a* of capital stock to output was smaller and the adjustment coefficient *b* for capital stock to reach equilibrium was also smaller before 1978.

In conclusion I have found that the permanent income hypothesis of Hall (1978) to explain consumption and the accelerations principle to explain investment are well supported by Chinese macro data for the periods 1952–1982 and 1987–2006 as well. This is one example of the applicability of economic theory to the Chinese economy. Other examples can be found in Chow (2007).

References

All China Data Center. (2009). "Foreign Trade and International Cooperation: Total Imports and Exports." *China Yearly Macro-Economic Statistics (National)*.

Chow, Gregory C. (1985). "A model of Chinese national income determination." *Journal of Political Economy*, 93, 782–792.

Chow, Gregory C. (2007). *China's Economic Transformation* (2nd ed). Blackwell.

Hall, Robert E. (1978). "Stochastic implications of the life-cycle-permanent income hypothesis: Theory and evidence." *Journal of Political Economy*, 86, 971–987.

CHAPTER 29

Lessons from Studying a Simple Macroeconomic Model for China*

In Chow (1985 and 2010) I found that aggregate consumption in China can be explained well by the permanent income hypothesis of Robert Hall and aggregate investment by the accelerations principle, using annual data from 1952 to 1982 and from 1978 to 2006 respectively. Updating Chow (2010) by including data from 2007 to 2009, this note finds (1) while the consumption equation continues to hold, the investment equation fails badly; (2) the investment equation continues to hold if data on investment for 2008 and 2009 is revised downward to reflect government expenditures as a part of the stimulus package during the world economic downturn; (3) small errors in one or two observations can reverse the sign of a significant regression coefficient in econometric practice.

I extend the data set of Chow (2010) by including observations from 2007 to 2009. Since the official data have been revised, the same method is used to obtain data from 1978 to 2009, as shown in Table 1. Note the differences between the data in Table 1 of Chow (2010) and Table 1 of this paper after revision.

First, I re-estimate the model using the revised data from 1987 to 2006 to find out whether data revision has changed the findings of Chow (2010). The estimated consumption and investment equations are shown in Eqs. (1)–(4) of Table 2. The method of estimation is

---

* Originally published in *Economics Letters*, 112 (2011), 233–235.

Table 1. Data on China's National Income and Its Determinants.

Year	Y	C	I	X	P
1978	3605.6	2239.1	1377.9	−11.4	1.000000
1979	4092.6	2633.7	1478.9	−20.0	1.054896
1980	4592.9	3007.9	1599.7	−14.7	1.098047
1981	5008.8	3361.5	1630.2	17.1	1.137821
1982	5590.0	3714.8	1784.2	91.0	1.164392
1983	6216.2	4126.4	2039.0	50.8	1.168060
1984	7362.7	4846.3	2515.1	1.3	1.201199
1985	9076.7	5986.3	3457.5	−367.1	1.305087
1986	10508.5	6821.8	3941.9	−255.2	1.388156
1987	12277.4	7804.6	4462.0	10.8	1.453466
1988	15388.6	9839.5	5700.2	−151.1	1.637111
1989	17311.3	11164.2	6332.7	−185.6	1.769748
1990	19347.8	12090.5	6747.0	510.3	1.904815
1991	22577.4	14091.9	7868.0	617.5	2.035899
1992	27565.2	17203.3	10086.3	275.6	2.175818
1993	36938.1	21899.9	15717.7	−679.5	2.558392
1994	50217.4	29242.2	20341.1	634.1	3.075802
1995	63216.9	36748.2	25470.1	998.6	3.490664
1996	74163.6	43919.5	28784.9	1459.2	3.722539
1997	81658.5	48140.6	29968.0	3549.9	3.750088
1998	86531.6	51588.2	31314.2	3629.2	3.685206
1999	91125.0	55636.9	32951.5	2536.6	3.606054
2000	98749.0	61516.0	34842.8	2390.2	3.603901
2001	109028.0	66933.9	39769.4	2324.7	3.674079
2002	120475.6	71816.5	45565.0	3094.1	3.721827
2003	136634.8	77685.5	55963.0	2986.3	3.836414
2004	160800.1	87552.6	69168.4	4079.1	4.101306
2005	187131.2	99051.3	77856.8	10223.1	4.287930
2006	222240.0	112631.9	92954.1	16654.0	4.519499
2007	265833.9	131510.1	110943.2	23380.6	4.735386
2008	314901.3	152346.6	138325.3	24229.4	5.116483
2009	345023.6	165526.8	164463.5	15033.3	5.137704

Sources: Y = GDP; C=consumption; I = investment; X = exports-imports, all in current prices, measured in 100 million RMB, and P is the GNP deflator constructed as the ratio of nominal GNP to GNP in constant prices given in *China Statistical Yearbook 2010*.

Table 2. Estimated Consumption and Investment Equations Including Data from 2007 to 2009.

Dependent variable	Y^*	Y_{-1}	(Y^*-Y_{-1})	C_{-1}	L_{-1}	Const	Sample ending in	R^2/s
(1) C	0.0418 (0.0359)			0.9829 (0.0720)		228.18 (102.79)	2006	0.9987/259.71
(2) C				1.0661 (0.0077)		168.89 (89.82)	2006	0.9986/261.45
(3) I	1.0057 (0.6804)	−0.8676 (0.6268)			0.5224 (0.3528)	−222.35 (156.87)	2006	0.9950/407.93
(4) I			0.2664 (0.5224)		1.0523 (0.1392)	−74.11 (131.77)	2006	0.9945/421.12
(5) C	0.0454 (0.0233)			0.9764 (0.0514)		232.67 (112.93)	2009	0.9990/290.88
(6) C				1.0758 (0.0068)		101.22 (94.90)	2009	0.9988/304.63
(7) I	−0.7512 (0.2099)	0.7074 (0.2180)			1.4467 (0.1305)	−130.34 (139.48)	2009	0.9979/392.59
(8) I	0.5159 (0.3210)	−0.4125 (0.2872)			0.7327 (0.2398)	−176.29 (145.84)	2007	0.9961/405.74
(9) I	−0.8703 (0.3993)	0.8092 (0.3650)			1.5213 (0.2464)	−117.77 (146.35)	2008	0.9971/399.88
(10) I	1.0201 (0.3086)	−0.8802 (0.2764)			0.5138 (0.2325)	−222.72 (143.41)	2007	0.9964/399.01
(11) I	1.4891 (0.3105)	−1.3328 (0.3040)			0.3502 (0.1719)	−239.35 (145.25)	2008	0.9970/403.67
(12) I	1.5572 (0.2799)	−1.3995 (0.2755)			0.3374 (0.1598)	−283.59 (143.19)	2009	0.9976/397.36

two-stage least squares as before, Y^* being the estimated regression of real GDP Y on Y_{-1}, C_{-1}, I_{-1} and X in the first stage. In the consumption Eq. (2) the insignificant Y^* is dropped. In investment Eq. (4), (Y^*-Y_{-1}) has replaced the two separate explanatory variables. The results show that the conclusions of Chow (2010) remain valid except that the support for the accelerations principle using the revised data is weaker. The standard errors of the coefficients of both Y^* and Y_{-1} in the investment equation (3) are large although these coefficients remain to have correct signs and expected orders of magnitude. The coefficient of (Y^*-Y_{-1}) in Eq. (4) has the correct sign but is insignificant. Using official data from 1978 to 2006 before revision the investment Eq. (3) in Chow (2010) has estimated coefficients of Y^* and Y_{-1} to be respectively 2.4149 and 2.2861 with standard errors of 0.6470 and 0.6281, providing stronger support for the accelerations principle.

Second, using data up to 2009 I find the consumption function to remain valid as shown in Eqs. (5) and (6) of Table 2. However, the investment equation, as shown in Eq. (7) of Table 2, fails to hold. In fact the coefficients of both Y^* and Y_{-1} have the wrong sign and are significant. I then check the failure by adding observations for one year at a time. The results are given in Eqs. (8) and (9) that include observations up to 2007 and up to 2008 respectively. Beginning in 2008 the signs of the coefficients of Y^* and Y_{-1} are wrong, as shown in Eqs. (9) and (7). Thus the accelerations principle fails for the years 2008 and 2009.

Third, I advance the following hypothesis to explain the failure of the investment equation. Note that 2008 was a special year when the Chinese government began applying a stimulus package to compensate for the slow growth in exports, and accordingly, the amount of investment recorded in official data is overestimated. The official data for C and I do not separate out government expenditures in these variables. The model is valid insofar as the determination of government expenditures as parts of C and I follows the same theoretical explanations as given in Chow (1985). Equations (9) and (7) show that this is not the case when a large stimulus package was introduced in 2008.

Fourth, I ask what investment figures for the two years 2008 and 2009 would need to be for the investment equation (3) estimated using data up to 2006 to remain valid. In this exercise I allow myself to move a part of I to the exogenous variable X in such a way that the official data for Y and C in the identity $Y = C + I + X$ remain unchanged. I have constructed artificial investment data for 2007, 2008 and 2009 by using the estimated investment equation (3) based on data up to 2006. In this construction the variable Y in the investment equation (3) means actual Y and not Y* as the latter serves to indicate the 2SLS method used to estimate this equation. Then I adjusted the variable X accordingly since the values of X are needed to perform the first stage of 2SLS in order to estimate Eqs. (10)–(12) of Table 2 using data up to 2007 to 2009 respectively. These three equations uphold the accelerations principle since the coefficients of Y* and Y_{-1} have the correct signs and correct relative orders of magnitudes and are all statistically significant.

The artificially constructed values of investment for years 2007 to 2009 are 115142.6, 131342.9 and 140395.7 (100 million RMB) as compared with the official data of 110943.2, 138325.3 and 164463.5 (100 million RMB) respectively. The 2007 figures are almost the same since the official investment data up to 2007 still support the accelerations principle as shown in Eq. (8). The constructed investment figure for 2008 is about 700 billion RMB less than the official figure. The constructed investment figure for 2009 is about 2400 billion RMB less than the official figure. These constructed investment figures are very reasonable as compared with the size of the government stimulus package of about 4 trillion RMB. Hence our hypothesis provides a satisfactory explanation of the failure of the estimated investment equation by using official investment data. We can thus accept the conclusion that the accelerations principle remains valid provided that the investment data are reasonably adjusted.

Finally, the above calculations provide an interesting example to show that small changes in the dependent variable for one or two observations in a sample of size 32 can change a regression coefficient from being significantly positive to being significantly negative.

Acknowledgement

The author would like to thank Yang Jin of the Wang Yanan Institute for Studies in Economics at Xiamen University for excellent research assistance in the preparation of this paper.

References

Chow, Gregory C. (1985). "A model of Chinese national income determination". *Journal of Political Economy*, 93, 782–792.

Chow, Gregory C. (2010). "Note on a model of Chinese national income determination". *Economic Letters*, 106, 195–196.

Hall, Robert E. (1978). "Stochastic implications of the life-cycle permanent income hypothesis: theory and evidence". *Journal of Political Economy*, 86, 971–987.

CHAPTER 30

Shanghai Stock Price Movements Reflecting China's Globalization

In this chapter I present one aspect of China's globalization in terms of its capital market by observing the movements of prices of stocks traded in the Shanghai stock market.

Investment is essential for economic development or increase in GDP. Stock markets are important for investment to take place. Economic globalization refers to the integration of the markets of different countries. Investors can choose to invest in different stocks traded in the stock markets of different countries. If world investors are optimistic about the stocks traded in a stock market of a certain country they will put their money in these stocks. If the investors are pessimistic they will sell these stocks. Such actions will affect the prices of the stocks in question. Stocks are first traded in the Shanghai stock market in 1990, at a time when the Chinese economy was not integrated with the world economy.

I once made study of the co-movements of the prices of stocks traded in the Shanghai Stock Market and the New York Stock Market, using weekly data from the beginning of 1992 to February 2002. Daily movements were not used because of the time difference between Shanghai and New York, with trades in Shanghai taking place before New York. Monthly movements are too long and miss the co-variation in the prices of stocks traded in the two markets. My study showed no co-movement in the prices in these two markets. I also predicted that co-movement would increase in the course of time following the integration of the Chinese economy into the world economy. This has already happened as shown by a recent investigation conducted by Professor Linlin Niu of the Wang Yanan Institute for Study in Economics of Xiamen University. This investigation is an update of my study using data up to the end of 2010.

I have used two variables to measure the movement of prices of stocks in the two markets. The first is the rate of return, which is the rate of change in the price during the week. The second is volatility, which is the absolute value of the rate of return. My study used weekly data from the first week of 1992 to the 8th week of 2002, with a total of 528 weeks, covering the co-movements in the rate of return and in the volatility of return as defined above.

I discovered that the average rate of return and the average volatility of the stocks traded in Shanghai were both higher than those traded in New York. While the correlation of the rates of return in the two markets was small (the correlation coefficient being −0.023), the correlation of the volatility measures was actually negative (the correlation coefficient being −0.121). Based on data from the beginning of February 2002 to the end of 2010, the above two correlation coefficients are respectively 0.152 and 0.258. The correlation coefficient 0.152 suggests that the rates of return in the two market tend to move together, although only to a limited extent. The corresponding correlation coefficient of the rates of returns for stocks traded in the Hong Kong and the New York stock markets from 1992 to the beginning of 2002 was already 0.396.

The investigation also finds that the volatility (defined as the absolute value of the rate of return) of prices of stocks traded in the Shanghai stock market has reduced, from 0.041 to 0.029 for the two periods mentioned above. For the same two periods, the volatility of prices of stocks traded in the New York stock market has increased from 0.015 to 0.019. This reflects the financial crisis in the US that occurred after 2007.

During the period from 1992 to 2002, the average rate of return of Shanghai stocks was higher than the average rate of New York stocks, being 17.5% per year as compared with 9.5%, before adjustment of inflation. During this period the annual inflation rates in the two countries were 5.3% and 2.6% respectively. Adjusted for inflation, the real rates of return to stocks traded in Shanghai and in New York became $17.5 - 5.3 = 12.2\%$ and $9.5 - 2.6 = 6.9\%$ respectively. Thus the real rate of return of stocks traded in Shanghai was higher than in New York by $12.2 - 6.9 = 5.3\%$ per year.

During the period after 2002, the average rates of return in both markets decreased as compared with the earlier period possibly because of the world financial crisis. Before adjusted for inflation the average rates of return of Shanghai and New York stocks were respectively 6.2% and 2.6% per year. Adjusted for the corresponding inflation rates of 2.5 and 2.4%, the real rates of return were 3.8% and 0.2%. Thus the real rate of return of Shanghai stocks was 3.6% higher than the New York stocks.

From 1992 to 2001 China's economy experienced a rapid rate of growth, affecting the rapid growth in demand for the stocks traded in the Shanghai stock market. This may explain the high rate of return for these stocks.

By observing the co-movement of prices of stocks traded in the Shanghai and the New York stock markets we can observe a part of the globalization of the Chinese economy.

CHAPTER 31

Co-Movements of Shanghai and New York Stock Prices by Time-Varying Regressions*

Time-varying regression is used to model the relationship between returns in Shanghai and New York stock markets. The parameters of the regressions reveal that the effect of current stock return of New York on Shanghai has been steadily increasing after the 1997 Asian financial crisis and turned significantly and persistently positive after 2002 when China entered WTO. The effect of current return of Shanghai on New York also became significantly positive and has been increasing after 2002. The upward trend of the effect has been interrupted during the recent global financial crisis, but reached the level of about 0.4–0.5 in 2010 for both markets. The results show that China's stock market has become more and more integrated to the world market in the past twenty years with interruptions occurring during the recent global economic downturn.

31.1. Introduction

The purpose of this paper is to study the co-movement of the price indices of stocks traded in the Shanghai and New York Stock

* Based on research jointly conducted with Liu Changjiang and Professor Niu Linlin of the Wang Yanan Institute for Study in Economics (WISE), Xiamen University and published in the *Journal of Comparative Economics*, 2011.

Exchanges by time-varying regressions. The parameters of the regressions will show the extent to which these two markets are integrated in the course of time. The estimates of the parameters are also measures of China's economic globalization, i.e., to what extent China's financial markets are affected by the US markets and to what extent the US markets are affected by the Chinese markets.

Globalization consists of flows of goods, capital, people and the accompanying information and technology among nations. After China opened up to the outside world in 1978, its economy has been gradually integrated to the rest of the world through international trade and foreign direct investment. This process has accelerated since China joined the WTO at the end of 2001. The flow of financial capital is an important component of globalization. China's capital market has experienced rapid development for twenty years since the Shanghai Stock Exchange was established in December 1990 and the Shenzhen Stock Exchange was founded one year later. As of the end of 2009, China's A-share market has become the world's second-largest after the United States, with a market value of 24.27 trillion RMB ($3.57 trillion). However, the extent to which China's financial market is internationally integrated into the world still remains a question and has not been adequately measured. For China, the flows of both physical capital, in the form of direct foreign investment, and financial capital are regulated by the government. There is a distinction between stocks traded in China which only the Chinese citizens can purchase (the A shares) and those which are reserved for foreigners (B shares).

In this paper we use time-varying regression to model the relationship between returns in the Shanghai and New York stock markets, with possible inclusion of lagged returns. The parameters of the regressions reveal the extent to which these two markets are integrated through time. Our econometric model implies a nonstationary relationship between the variables for China and for the outside world. Under such circumstances, a cointegration test assuming long run equilibrium is inappropriate to find the trend of integration. Likewise, by assuming the existence of an unconditional covariance matrix of returns, multivariate GARCH models or

stochastic volatility models assume stationarity and tend to emphasize high frequency changes in volatility and covolatility but ignore
the underlying smooth structural change model in this paper. In
spite of the institutional restrictions in China's financial market, we
find robust evidence of a steady increase of integration between the
Shanghai and New York stock markets, with the integration becoming particularly stronger after China joined the WTO. The process
was disturbed during the recent financial crisis, but the trend was
restored in 2010.

I first present in Sec. 2 a comparison of the regressions of the rate
of return and of volatility of stocks traded in the Shanghai Stock
Exchange on the corresponding variables for the New York Stock
exchange in the two periods 1992–2002 and 2002–2010. In Sec. 3
I present three specifications of models of regressions with time-
varying parameters to study the co-movement between the rates of
return of stocks traded in the Shanghai and New York stock markets.
The results of estimating these models are given in Sec. 4. The results
show that the method of regression with time-varying parameters
depicts the co-movements of the stock prices in the two markets
extremely well. These results agree with the history of China's globalization and of the recent world economic downturn during the
period studied. Section 5 concludes.

31.2. Co-Movement of Prices of Stocks Traded in the Shanghai and New York Stock Exchanges in Two Sample Periods

Stocks were first traded in the Shanghai stock market in December
1990, at a time when the Chinese economy was not integrated
with the world economy. Chow and Lawler (2003) studied the co-
movements of the prices of stocks traded in the Shanghai Stock
Market and the New York Stock Market, using weekly data from the
beginning of 1992 to February 2002. Daily movements were not
used because of the time difference between Shanghai and New York,
with trades in Shanghai taking place before New York. Monthly inter-
vals are too long and miss the co-variation in the prices of stocks

traded in the two markets. Chow and Lawler (2003) used two variables to measure the weekly movement of prices of stocks in the two markets. The first is the rate of return r_t, which is the rate of change in weekly prices, calculated as log difference of price: $\ln(P_t) - \ln(P_t)$. The second is volatility, which is measured by the absolute value of the rate of return $|r_t|$. The study showed no co-movement in the prices in these two markets and predicted that co-movement would increase in the course of time following the integration of the Chinese economy into the world economy.

In this section I examine weekly returns of Shanghai and New York stocks for two subsamples. The first is from 1992-01-27 to 2002-02-25 as in Chow and Lawler (2003), and the second is from 2002-03-04 to 2010-12-27, with 511 and 455 observations respectively, after excluding holidays on either market with missing data. For the entire sample the beginning of 2002 is a reasonable break point. The two stock price indices used in Chow and Lawler (2003) and in this paper are the Shanghai Composite Index and the NYSE Composite Index, as reported in Datastream International. The two subsamples divide the sample roughly into halves. China joined WTO at the end of 2001 which promotes the economic and financial integration of China's financial market into the world financial market.

For the whole sample and each subsample, Table 1 presents summary statistics of returns and volatilities (measured by absolute return). Table 2 compares correlations of the two measures between the two markets.

From the above two tables, three observations are in order.

1. Overall, the mean and variance of the Shanghai Stock return are higher.

2. During the first subsample before February 2002, Shanghai stock return experienced a highly volatile period due to its early development stage and the 1997 Asian crisis. During the recent financial crisis in 2007–2008, the New York stock return experienced a surge in volatility; while the Shanghai stock volatility was affected to some extent, the change in volatility is not as drastic as the New York counterpart.

Table 1. Rate of Return and Volatility in the Full Sample and Two Subsamples.

	Shanghai rate of return			New York rate of return		
	Full sample	Before Feb. 2002	After Feb. 2002	Full sample	Before Feb. 2002	After Feb. 2002
Mean	0.002308	0.003095	0.001405	0.001245	0.001846	0.000554
Variance	0.0037	0.075292	0.038073	0.000630	0.019708	0.030129

	Shanghai volatility			New York volatility		
	Full sample	Before Feb. 2002	After Feb. 2002	Full sample	Before Feb. 2002	After Feb. 2002
Mean	0.035455	0.041297	0.028748	0.016823	0.014644	0.019326
Variance	0.002449	0.063005	0.024964	0.000348	0.013303	0.023103

Table 2. Correlation of Rate of Return and Volatility.

	Rate of return		
	Full sample	Before Feb. 2002	After Feb. 2002
Correlation	0.041632	−0.022727	0.151953

	Volatility		
	Full sample	Before Feb. 2002	After Feb. 2002
Correlation	0.000598	−0.120583	0.257922

3. The correlation of returns between the two markets turned from negative before 2002 to positive after. This happened both in terms of return and its absolute value, a proxy for volatility. The negative correlation before 2002 was explained in Chow and Lawler (2003) as driven by macro fundamentals which were different in the two countries. The positive correlation after 2002 reflects economic and financial integration through time.

In what follows, I regress return of one market on its own lag term and on the current and lagged returns of the other market. For

Table 3.　Regressions of Rate of Return of Shanghai and New York Stock Indices.

Lag	Shanghai			New York		
	All data (obs. 955)	Before 02.2002 (obs. 510)	After 02.2002 (obs. 444)	All data (obs. 955)	Before 02.2002 (obs. 510)	After 02.2002 (obs. 444)
	Coef./t	Coef./t	Coef./t	Coef./t	Coef./t	Coef./t
S0				0.0225	−0.0057	0.1368
				1.68	−0.49	3.63*
S1	0.1090	0.1235	0.0337	−0.0260	−0.0036	−0.1172
	3.38	2.80	0.72	−1.94	−0.31	−3.16*
N0	0.1318	−0.0828	0.2131			
	1.68	−0.49	3.63*			
N1	0.1675	−0.0259	0.2614	−0.0880	−0.1240	−0.0845
	2.14	−0.15	4.46*	−2.73	−2.80	−1.77
Cons.	0.0017	0.0029	0.0009	0.0014	0.0021	0.0006
	0.85	0.86	0.52	1.70	2.43	0.40
R^2	0.0189	0.0158	0.0684	0.0138	0.0159	0.0546
RMSE	0.0604	0.0750	0.0367	0.0250	0.0196	0.0294

Shanghai the lag terms are selected first by AIC for the first subsample in order to be comparable to the Chow and Lawler (2003) subsample. Then we do the same regression for the full sample and the other subsample in order to see the difference between different periods. In Table 3, the first column displays variable names, where "S" stands for Shanghai and "N" stands for New York, the number 0 and 1 denote lag orders. For each coefficient, we report the t-statistics behind it.

From the multivariate regressions in Table 3 for returns, it is evident that after 2002, the interaction between markets was stronger. A star indicates that the return of the foreign market has a significant effect. It can be seen that not only the lagged and current values of returns from the New York market affect the corresponding variables in Shanghai, but the effects also go from the Shanghai to the New York market.

31.3. Specification of Time-Varying Coefficient Regressions for the Co-Movement between Stock Returns in Shanghai and New York

As revealed by the statistics and linear regressions presented in the last section, there have been significant structural changes in the co-movement of returns in the Shanghai and New York stock market. In this section we specify three time-varying coefficient regressions of the rate of return of one market on the return of the other market. In a bivariate distribution there are two regressions. Movements in the New York Stock Exchange represent a larger part of the global financial activities than movements in the Shanghai Stock Exchange. To reflect possible asymmetric effects between these two markets, we run the regressions in both directions. In each specification, the time-varying coefficient of the current foreign market return is modeled as a random walk process. The model of random walk is appropriate because an autoregression coefficient of less than unity would imply a stationary process with the parameter converging to a constant.

Three specifications of the regressions for co-movement between the Shanghai and New York stock returns have been examined. The first specification is the simplest one where return in domestic market is regressed only on the foreign return with a constant intercept and a time-varying coefficient. The second specification adds one lagged domestic return with constant coefficient to the first specification. The third specification adds to the second specification one lagged foreign return as an additional independent variable with a time-varying coefficient. This choice of a time-varying coefficient reflects the subsample comparison in Table 3 of Section 2 for those coefficients which change signs and are significant for the second subsample. These time-varying coefficient models fit naturally into the state-space framework. The states here are the time-varying parameters. Standard maximum likelihood estimation (MLE) with the Kalman filter can be used to estimate the models.

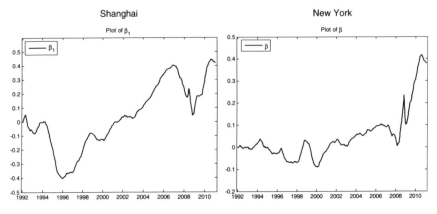

Figure 1.   Plot of β_t

31.4. Estimation Results

This section presents the parameter estimates of each model for both market returns. For the constant coefficients, I report the estimates in the equation and denote the t-statistics in parentheses; for time-varying coefficients, I plot the estimated time-varying coefficient through time in Fig. 1.

Model I:

$$r_t^{sh} = 0.0026(1.0454) + \beta_t r_t^{ny} + e_t$$

$$r_t^{ny} = 0.0012(0.9337) + \beta_t r_t^{sh} + e_t$$

From the first equation and the first plot we observe how the New York market influences the Shanghai market. In this simplest specification, the effect of the current stock return of New York on Shanghai, measured by β_t, has been steadily increasing after the 1997 Asian crisis. The impact turns to significantly and persistently positive after 2002 when China entered WTO. The upward trend has been interrupted during the recent financial crisis, but in 2010 it resumed the level before crisis as the markets gradually recovered from the financial and economic turmoil.

From the second equation and Fig. 2 we observe how the Shanghai market influences the New York market. The effect of Shanghai on New York was weaker as expected and was close to zero before 2002. The impact became positive and has been increasing since 2002, but it reversed direction during the financial crisis, and then increases rapidly in 2009 and 2010.

Overall, it is clear that the co-movement between Shanghai and New York stock returns became positively related and stronger in the past decade, with interruptions associated with the global financial market turmoil.

Model II:

$$r_t^{sh} = 0.0021(1.0852) + \beta_t r_t^{ny} + 0.0975(0.3502)r_{t-1}^{sh} + e_t,$$

$$r_t^{ny} = 0.0014(1.0030) + \beta_t r_t^{sh} + 0.0843(0.5573)r_{t-1}^{ny} + e_t.$$

From the results of the second model where an autoregressive part is added to explain the domestic return, the paths of the time-varying coefficients for the two markets are fairly similar to the paths of the first model as shown in Fig. 2. The effect of the New York market on the Shanghai market has been stronger than the effect in the opposite direction. Both coefficients turned persistently positive after

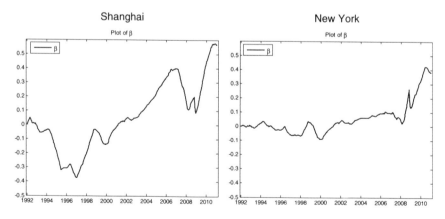

Figure 2.   Plot of β_t

2002. After the financial crisis, the coefficient resumed a high value of about 0.4–0.5.

Model III:

$$r_t^{sh} = 0.0026(1.1818) + \beta_{1,t}r_t^{ny} - 0.0103(-0.2959)r_{t-1}^{sh} + \beta_{2,t}r_{t-1}^{ny} + e_t$$

$$r_t^{ny} = 0.0013(0.9286) + \beta_{1,t}r_t^{sh} - 0.0103(-1.0862)r_{t-1}^{ny} + \beta_{2,t}r_{t-1}^{sh} + e_t$$

To further check the robustness for the time-varying coefficients of the current returns of the foreign market, we add one lagged foreign market return also with a time-varying coefficient. This specification is motivated by the results of estimation presented in Sec. 2, where we have found the coefficient of the lagged foreign return becoming statistically insignificant in the latter subsample.

The results as illustrated in Figs. 3 and 4 show that:

1. The coefficients of the current foreign returns are still robust with the presence of the lag variable, showing paths similar in shape to those based on Models I and II.

2. Conditional on the impact of the current foreign returns, the effects of the lagged foreign returns are less important. For Shanghai, lagged New York return seems to have positive effects around 1994 while the

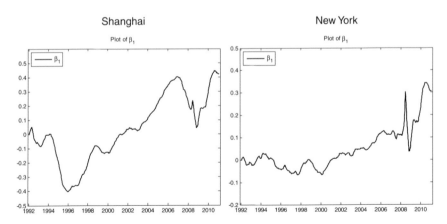

Figure 3.   Plot of β_{1t}

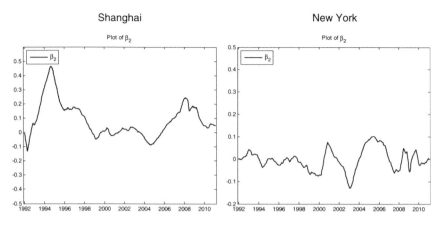

Figure 4. Plot of β_{2t}

effect of current return is zero or negative, indicating that the information in New York return may affect Shanghai stock price with some time lag. But with β_{1t} turning significantly positive after 2002, β_{2t} becomes closer to zero while remaining positive most of the time.

3. For New York, conditional on the presence of β_{1t}, β_{2t} is not significantly different from zero, showing the weak lagged effect of the Shanghai market.

31.5. Conclusion

By the use of time-varying regressions, this paper has provided estimates of the degrees of dependence of the Shanghai stock market on the New York market and the dependence in the opposite direction. Weekly estimates are provided from January 1992 to December 2010. The time-varying coefficients obtained by regressing current returns of Shanghai (New York) on New York (Shanghai) are fairly robust among alternative specifications.

As Figure 1 shows, the effect of current stock return of New York on Shanghai has been steadily increasing after the 1997 Asian crisis and turned significantly and persistently positive after 2002 when China entered WTO. For New York, it is also the case that the effect of current return of Shanghai becomes significantly positive and increasing after 2002. The upward trend has been disturbed during the recent financial crisis, but the coefficient reaches the level of about 0.4–0.5 in 2010 for both markets. China's stock market has become more and more integrated to the world market in the past twenty years. Our results provide measures of this integration.

It remains the task of future research to build models to explain the process of economic globalization itself with China and the US playing important roles.

Reference

Chow, Gregory C. and C.C. Lawler. (2003). "A time series analysis of Shanghai and New York stock price indices." *Annals of Economics and Finance*, 4, 17–35.

Index